RESETOLOGY

RESETOLOGY™
Calming and Connecting Secrets from the Principal's Office

JIM HOUSE

Jim House
619-990-9312
Jim@Resetology.com
Resetology.com

Resetology™: Calming and Connecting Secrets from the Principal's Office

Copyright © 2014 by James House

ISBN: 978-0-692-27824-6

www.Resetology.com

All feedback welcome! Please find the contact information on the website. Thanks.

DEDICATION

To my dad who posted "No Robbers Allowed" signs around our apartment so that I could fall sleep unafraid in second grade; and to my mom who packed our lunch and took us on field trips to watch giant tractors move dirt around, and who nurtured our imaginations with a nightly regimen of Charlie, Willy, James, and Danny from the pages of Dahl's magical stories.

Contents

Foreword

Clichés reveal many of our private thoughts as parents:

- My kids mean everything to me....
   Of course they do.
- If I could start over again as a parent I'd do things differently....
   It's never too late to do things differently.
- You only get one chance to make a first impression....
   But loving your kids is filled with second and third attempts.
- Things are different now than when I was growing up....
   No they aren't.
- Kids don't come with a manual....
   Read this book — THIS is your manual!

In the Air Force, through 20 years as a salesman, and as father of seven children, I've learned that people are predictable and that Newton was right: "When one body exerts a force on a second body, the second body simultaneously exerts a force equal in magnitude and opposite in direction on the first body."

Your kids give back to you exactly what you give to them, and that's our problem. The busyness and the stress of life leads you to respond to your children in a less-than-loving way more times than we'd like to admit. It's not that we don't love them, but:

- "If I told them once...."
- "These kids think money grows on trees...."
- "They think electricity is free...."
- "These dishes aren't going to wash themselves...."
- "All they do is fight. Just ONE night I'd like my kids to get along."

You know how the rest of the day is going to go from that point onward. It doesn't have to be that way.

You can have less stress and more peace in your household starting today with the lessons, the strategies, and the tactics you will learn in this book.

This is not pop psychology or brute force. It's not a bunch of mumbo jumbo or theoretical role-playing written to make the author feel better about himself. The principles behind Resetology™ have been honed over decades by a master educator who has spent his life educating, counseling, and diffusing stressful situations with kids.

I have already seen it work in my household. I guarantee it will work for you. But first you need to buy this book!

May you "reset" in peace.

—Wes Schaeffer
The Sales Whisperer®
Author of The Definitive Guide to Infusionsoft and
It Takes More Than a Big Smile, a Good Idea &
a Twitter Account to Build a Business That Lasts

OPENING

CHAPTER 1

There's Always Another Way

A N OVER-SIZED EIGHTH GRADER STORMED THROUGH MY DOOR A STEP ahead of his security escort. A lunchtime conflict had landed him in my office. He dropped aggressively into the open chair and white-knuckled the armrests in defiance.

"I didn't do it!" he yelled with the added volume that middle-schoolers often think will add credibility to their story. I let him rant and then I said a few words.

"Wha –" he said, his face contorted with confusion.

I let him continue his story and then I injected a few more words.

He paused as a smile threatened to emerge.

One minute later we were calmly discussing his actions and consequences.

Does that sound impossible? Have you ever wished you had the ability to quickly calm your own children?

Here is an account shared by a working dad with four boys.

had just finished chauffeuring the boys back from practices, and was trying to finish up some work for a big, national client that I needed to email before dinner. I had managed to get the older boys to start their homework when Mikey, my youngest, decided that he had to go play at the neighbor's house – now. He was ignoring me and he was whining incessantly. So I got up from the table.

"Mike, Mike, hey Mikey, let's try this ..."

One minute later Mikey went off to play in his room with a big smile on his face. And I was able to finish my work.

Let me ask again. Does that sound impossible? Have you ever wished you had that ability to quickly calm your own children?

Have you ever thought:

➡ I'm tired of having to repeat myself.
➡ I'm tired of having to raise my voice to get a response.
➡ I just wish I could get them to listen without having to get angry.

You may have wondered, "Am I a good parent?" Well, I *know* you're a good parent because you're reading this book, and you've read other parenting books, and you are deeply involved in your kids' lives. But there are still plenty of times when you feel helpless; maybe you even resent your kids sometimes.

I struggled with many of these same issues as a first-year teacher — and almost failed. But then I discovered and developed some powerful yet simple techniques that changed everything. These techniques worked like magic. Let me explain.

Many years ago I found my ideal career. I had finally discovered what I was meant to do with my life, the perfect vocation to use all of my God-given gifts to really help kids. I had just completed my training as a teacher, and I was super excited about it. I had studied hard, I had prepared hard, and I was at the top of my class.

I landed the job of my dreams in the district of my dreams. In that district your principal did not evaluate you during your first year. Instead, you were observed and evaluated by a mentor teacher, who would ultimately give you the thumbs up or down at the end of your first year — or sooner.

The mentor teacher came in to observe me in the classroom several times, and then we had our first observation conference. I was very excited about the conference. I loved the kids and the job and I was looking forward to hearing great things — about me! I honestly imagined her saying, "Jim, you're amazing. You're a natural! We are so grateful that you chose to grace the teaching profession with your skills, and thank you for coming to teach in our district!"

As it happened, the first words out of her mouth were, "Your principal and I are worried about your classroom management."

My heart stopped. My head got warm and my whole body began to sweat. She could not have said anything more shocking or more devastating to me. My entire being flooded with fear because when she said those words, in my mind I heard her say, "You're fired! You failed!"

My beautiful new life was collapsing around me. My friends knew how thrilled I was to be a teacher and had watched me work hard for years to prepare for this. They were on this journey with me. My parents were both former educators, and they were so proud of me. They were on this journey with me, too. I wanted so much to impress them all, and in that instant I was suffocating with humiliation and shame. This was the opposite of what I had expected, so I listened to the rest of her words in a state of shock.

I had started the year by sitting my students in small groups and had them working together on several activities throughout the day. Where I saw students having fun while learning, my mentor saw chaos. I was a brand new teacher and definitely needed coaching, but instead of guiding me through specific changes that I needed to make to improve my classroom management, she directed me to structure and manage the class in an extreme way that was the polar opposite of everything I had been doing.

She had me put all of the desks in rows with the kids facing forward. There were no more group activities, just lots of individual seatwork. Lots of "drill and kill"! Every instruction now sounded like, "Turn to page 83 and read the chapter. Then complete the stack of worksheets." Literally.

It was killing the kids — and it was killing me! I was miserable. But I had to do it her way or lose my job. Every time I saw that mentor teacher approaching my classroom, my heart would race and I would feel the panic run up the back of my neck. My future was in her hands. I didn't want to quit, but I seriously considered it. This was certainly not what I had thought teaching was going to be like for me.

The breakthrough came unexpectedly a few months later. I was leaving the teachers' lounge and I had an entire group of teachers laughing as we spilled out the door. The principal put his hand on my shoulder to get my attention, and said quietly, "You know, Jim, I wonder if there is a way that you can bring some of your personality into the classroom?"

That was all he said and then he walked away. But I began to wonder, "Could there really be another way?" I realized that there *had* to be another way! Another way to effectively manage students' emotions, behavior, attention, and moods — that wouldn't kill us all!

Hope entered my life in that moment and I became excited, curious, and determined, all at once. I began to look at my classroom in a different way. I realized that I had some God-given gifts for connecting with kids in an endless array of situations. I began to pay very close attention to what captured and held my students' attention. I started to experiment with ways to manage students' behavior that were more engaging for both the students and for me. And that's how I ended up creating the techniques that gave birth to Resetology™.

These new techniques led me to be very successful as a teacher, and two years later, I was giving workshops in the district to impart the methods I had developed to other teachers — including all of the new teachers in the district.

A few years later when I became a middle-school vice principal in a gang-riddled neighborhood, I modified my classroom techniques so that I could use them in the office to quickly calm irate and uncooperative students.

Over the years, as the principal of several tough schools, using the Resetology™ techniques allowed me to be hugely successful with thousands of poorly behaved kids. Kids of every sort, from violent gang kids to wonderful kids just like yours who, even though they are growing up in a loving and nurturing home, can still drive you crazy.

As a principal, I had daily conversations with parents who were frustrated by their kids' behavior. Parents frustrated that parenting was not what they thought it was going to be.

Has parenting turned out to be different than you imagined it would be? Do you ever think to yourself, "This is not what I signed up for"? I have been training parents in Resetology™ seminars and as coaching clients for several years, and I hear that sentiment frequently from the parents I work with.

I found a different and better way. If there were a different and better way open for you, would you try it?

Resetology™ gives parents like you the confidence and ability to quickly calm your kids, transform their irritating moods, and connect in the fun ways you've always longed for.

Let's take some of the frustrating situations you find yourself tackling with your child on a regular basis. You want him to do his homework, or take out the trash, or practice his piano, but he is ignoring you. So what do you do?

If you are like most parents I've worked with, you tell your child a couple of times, maybe you even give him a warning, and when he still doesn't respond you end up raising your voice to get him to act.

"The feeling is that you are out of options," one dad shared with me. He continued:

> I start saying the craziest stuff like, "I work all day at my job, and you know why? To make money to take care of you, that's why. To pay for this house. And Mom works all day and she makes your lunch for school." I know it's dumb and won't help, but I'm out of ideas.

Another parent said to me, "We all get to the point where we say to our kids the things our parents said to us, which we swore we would never say to our kids."

Because Resetology™ worked so powerfully, consistently, and easily with kids in schools, I figured it had to work for parents, as well. Resetology™ was developed based on thousands of data sets, from countless different situations, with every kind of kid imaginable, and it worked with all of them.

Any concerns I may have had about how well Resetology™ would transfer over to family life vanished when I began to talk with "über moms" about this book. They pinned me down in long conversations, grilling me excitedly for the details of how I used Resetology™ in schools. Again and again I heard, "I've read the parenting books — and there is nothing like this out there!"

Your goal, my goal, Resetology™'s goal — they are all the same. Get a child, your child, to start — or stop — doing something without having to reach for the nuclear option! It goes deeper than that, though: to calm the child quickly, transform their undesirable mood, and positively connect with them in a way that builds toward your future together. And isn't that what you want?

For 14 years I used Resetology™ at schools on a daily basis to coax stubborn students into class, to engage unmotivated students with their learning, and to resolve volatile playground disputes, all while connecting with those kids — especially those who were frequently in trouble.

You can approach Resetting with the confidence of knowing that loads of parents have already gotten the results you desire with their own kids.

And I personally have used Resetters successfully with literally thousands of kids, of all ages, within the entire range of emotional intensity. Resetology™ is not theoretical, or experimental, or untested. Resetology™ is sound and proven. And it WILL work when YOU use it with your own kids, too.

Here is just a taste of what others are saying:

> Dear Jim:
>
> I can't possibly overstate how helpful and effective your Resetology™ is. Not only has it helped tremendously in defusing situations and overcoming conflict with my children, but it also has proven to be an effective method for me to deal with conflict and difficult situations in all aspects of my life, so long as I remember to use it. To be completely candid, it also is teaching me to take a step back before reacting or, worse, overreacting.
>
> — *Maria,* Mom of 3

> It totally deflated the situation, very simply and very quickly, which frankly was exactly what I need because when you have four boys, you need to be able to defuse things pretty quickly. I find Resetology™ to be a simple method that offers a quick solution, and I really appreciate it.
>
> — *Robert,* Dad of 4

> As a successful parent of two grown boys — men, now — I attended a Resetology™ seminar out of curiosity at the invitation of a friend. When it was over I was envious of the young parents in the room! As my sons were growing up I could have used these secrets so many times.
>
> Instead of having to "rebuild the engine" because I waited too long, with Resetology™ it would have been like a shot of WD-40 in the right place at the right time. Resetology™ is WD-40 for parents! Can't wait to use it with my grandkids!
>
> — *John,* Dad of 2

Here's what awaits you in the rest of this book. I present Resetology in three modules — Preset, Reset™, and Mindset:

The Preset

A super-simple look at how emotions work, presented with the help of a common kitchen metaphor. It will prepare you to positively impact your child's emotions.

The Reset

Step-by-step training on how to quickly calm kids and transform their undesirable moods.

The Mindset

An insider's guide to connecting with your kids – specifically, how to strengthen, repair, and restore relationships with your children. The Mindset helps you to fulfill the two long-term goals of Resetology™:

➡ teaching your kids how to manage their own emotional state at all times (an essential life skill for creating and maintaining connection)

➡ establishing life-long, loving relationships with your kids and between your kids, which will be passed on to their future spouses – and your future grandchildren!

I am thrilled and honored to share calming secrets from the principal's office with you.

Remember, **there's always another way!**

PRESET
RESET
MINDSET

CHAPTER 2
Let's Talk Cookies!

EMOTIONS 101

EMOTIONS ARE NOT AS COMPLEX AS YOU MIGHT THINK. IN THIS CHAPTER I AM going to use the analogy of a simple cookie recipe to teach you how your emotions work, so you can successfully transform the undesirable emotions of your own children. So, let's talk cookies!

My Great Aunt Nettie used to bake cookies for us when she visited at Christmas time every year. The cookies were amazing — especially the sugar cookies drenched with a heavenly orange glaze. Every year she would stuff us with batches of six or seven different types of cookies. Each cookie she made had its own unique recipe. She had long since memorized the recipes, and they always came out of the oven with the exact same *über*-goodness. Every time.

Emotions are very similar to cookies. Each emotion has a specific recipe. When I am sad, I "bake" the sad recipe the same way every time. When I'm happy, I "bake" the happy recipe the same way. Every time. You do too, and so do your children.

Aunt Nettie's cookies were delicious beyond description, yet there were really only two kinds of ingredients in each of her recipes: wet ingredients and dry ingredients.

Cookie Recipe = wet ingredients + dry ingredients

And just as cookies have two kinds of ingredients — wet and dry — there are also just two basic ingredients in every emotion: focus and physiology. Each emotion we experience is composed of a precise combination of these two ingredients. Let's call this an "emotion recipe."

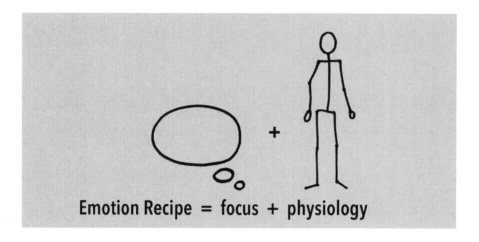

Emotion Recipe = focus + physiology

Now let's look at how these two ingredients are combined to create the recipe for the emotions.

The Recipe for Sad

What do you think about when you are sad? (Focus)
You focus on thoughts that are negative.

Focus for sad:
"Why does this always happen to me?"
"I can't believe this happened again."

What do you look like when you are sad? (Physiology)
Chances are pretty good that you drop your chin towards your chest, droop your shoulders, and begin to breathe shallowly; your face is cloudy with a chance of tears.

Physiology for sad:
Chin down, droopy posture, tears

Notice now how the ingredients (focus and physiology) change as the emotion changes.

The Recipe for Happy

What do you think about when you are happy? (Focus)

These are typical thoughts you focus on when you are happy:

Focus for happy:
"She loves me!"
"I LOVE my life!"

What do you look like when you are happy? (Physiology)

You probably have a big grin on your face, your head is held high, and you may be jumping up and down or moving in an animated way.

Physiology for happy:
Big toothy grin, with head and chest held high!

FOCUS POCUS

Let's take a deeper look into focus and physiology because understanding these two ingredients is critical to knowing how to transform undesirable emotions.

Focus is simply the thoughts or objects that we pay particular attention to in any moment.

Focus = thoughts we pay attention to

Try this short exercise: read and follow the directions below.

Pay attention to the feeling of your feet inside your shoes.

PAUSE.

Notice the feeling of the clothes against your skin.

PAUSE.

Become aware of the sounds in the space around you.

PAUSE.

Feel the breath flowing in and out of your nose and mouth.

PAUSE.

If you are like most people, you were not aware of any of these sensations until you read each line. But as soon as you focused on each sensation you instantly became aware of it. More importantly, you were no longer paying attention to whatever it was you had been thinking of before you changed your focus. And since the thoughts you focus on comprise one half of the recipe for the emotion you feel, it is critical to *pay attention to what holds your attention.*

Most people do not pay attention to the thoughts that race through their own minds. In every moment there is a dizzying myriad of thoughts you can focus on from your past, present, or future.

Thought from the past:
"I still can't believe she said that."
"That was the best kiss of my life!"

Thoughts from the present:
"I'm so proud of you!"
"I love this song!"

Thoughts from the future:
"I am never going to finish this in time."
"I can't wait for dinner tonight!"

Whichever thoughts you choose to focus on will greatly influence your emotional state. The same is true for children. If you guide a child to change what they focus on, you can lead them to change their emotional state.

PHYSIOLOGY

> Motion creates emotion.
> *— Tony Robbins*

The second ingredient of the emotion recipe is physiology. Physiology involves everything having to do with our bodies, including posture, facial expression, breathing, and vocal expression.

Physiology = posture, facial expression, voice, breathing

You're watching a TV show with your family. A phone rings and one of your family members steps outside to take the call. She's standing on the other side of the sliding glass door and after a few seconds she stands up straighter and her face suddenly explodes into a big smile.

Even though you can't hear what she is saying, can you guess what emotion she is experiencing? You're right! She's happy, or excited, or thrilled. You may have given her emotion a different name, but you knew that she was experiencing something very positive.

While we can't tell what someone is thinking just by looking at them, we can see what's going on with much of their physiology. Physiology is the obvious ingredient in the emotion recipe. Physiology usually broadcasts our emotions for anyone to see.

While it is obvious that emotions often dictate physiology, the reverse is just as true: *changing physiology changes emotions.*

I think you know this intuitively—certainly most mothers do. As a child, I would approach my mom with one of many serious laments:

> Mom, I'm bored....
>
> There's nothing to do....

My wise mother would invariably respond, "Why don't you go outside and run around?" I loved to run and she knew that as soon as I got outside it would not be long before I was running ... running to fill my billowing superhero cape with enough wind to lift me high above the city, or running to commence a full-blown pirate attack upon some unsuspecting pirate ship. And in a matter of minutes, even seconds, my mood was improved because I was being physically active. My mom got me to change my physiology and in doing so she changed my mood.

But what my mom did not know is that even small, subtle changes in physiology can quickly lead to a positive change in emotion.

Change the Recipe!

Let's circle back to Aunt Nettie's cookies. Let's say I want to bake some of those delicious cookies myself. What would happen if I changed the recipe a bit? I could ruin the recipe by removing the baking soda, but I could also make it better by substituting imported Swiss chocolate chips. Either way, by altering the ingredients I change the recipe. If I change the cookie recipe, I'm going to end up with a different cookie. The same is true of emotions.

Change either of the ingredients (focus or physiology) and you change the emotion recipe. Change the emotion recipe and you end up with a different emotion. That's the crux of "resetting". Here is the secret resetting formula:

> **Change the ingredient ➡ Change the emotion recipe**
>
> **Change the emotion recipe ➡ Change the emotion**

Just as it is possible to ruin a batch of cookies by using the wrong ingredients, it is also possible to worsen a child's emotional state — by losing your temper or yelling. So, in order to avoid that, I'm also going to teach you how to use Resetology™ to positively change your own emotion recipe first, so you don't say something you may later regret.

I know what some of you are thinking — you think I'm talking about distraction, like jangling keys in front of a baby. Stay with me. It's much more than that. This is purposeful, planned, often rehearsed, and it yields both short- and long-term outcomes for you and your children that far surpass simple diversion.

So just how do you "reset" your child's focus or physiology? I'm glad you asked! I'm going to equip you with some simple, powerful, and proven techniques in the next section. You can do this!

CHAPTER 3

Pssst…
Your Kid is a Navy SEAL

T HERE ARE THREE THINGS GOING ON INSIDE YOUR KID'S HEAD THAT YOU NEED to be aware of, because it's the awareness of three things that make Resetology™ so powerful.

These same three things are active in the mind of every child — young or old, consistently well-behaved or challenging, kids who are fortunate to have great parents like you and kids who live dangerous lives in the shadow-fringes of our towns. Let's take a quick look at one of these hardened kids living a life that no child should ever be exposed to.

MICHELANGELO

Eddie, a big, slow-moving eighth grader, was new on campus, but his intimidating presence had already sent ripples through the pre-existing hierarchy of tough guys. He had kept himself off of the discipline radar until this particular morning when he was accused of vandalizing a teacher's car. He now sat in my office.

"You do understand that I'm going to have to suspend you, don't you? And I have to call the police."

He remained silent and stared back at me with the wrong kind of confidence — the kind that boasted, "This ain't nothing."

"Eddie," I continued, "I don't think you did it. But unless you give me some new information I won't have any choice."

He remained politely defiant. His eyes wandered around the room and paused on me, calculating.

His protective armor was formidable and I knew it was going to be nearly impossible for me to break through. I needed to get him to take the armor off himself. It was time to try something wildly unexpected.

I pulled one of my art history books from the shelf and opened up to a large photo of Michelangelo's *Pieta*. I held it out to him and said, "A guy named Michelangelo carved this out of one big rock hundreds of years ago — see how soft the drapes in her robe look."

He turned his head toward the page, squinted to focus, and then took the book and laid it in his own lap. He gently traced the photo with his fingers as if trying to feel the softness in the stone. When he handed the book back, I turned to a photo of Jan van Eyck's *Arnolfini Portrait* and said, "Check out the wooden shoes." He took the book more easily and examined the painting. When he looked up, I said, "Look at the chandelier." He gave that some serious attention, and after a moment I said,

"Look at the reflection in the mirror."

His gaze traveled slowly to the mirror in the picture, and then after an instant his head shot forward to give it closer inspection. I knew he had discovered what the painter had hidden in the mirror's reflection. I wouldn't say that Eddie actually smiled, but the corners of his mouth betrayed that he wanted to. Finally, he closed the book, gently handed it back to me, and then answered my previous questions without any additional prompting from me.

Turns out I was right — he hadn't done it.

So how did I get this hardened and uncooperative teen to open up to me? To answer that, I'm going to reveal to you the three things that are always running in the background of kids' daily interactions. Like the operating system on your computer, this triad of thoughts forms the hidden logic that powers what you see on your screen. Once you are aware of these three things, you'll understand why Resetology™ works so well. Here they are:

1. Your kids are watching.
2. Your kids are certain that they know how you will act.
3. Your kids are certain that they can outsmart you.

We are going to take a deeper look at how these operate in your own kids' lives, but first let's go back and apply this triad to the Michelangelo story above.

1. Your kids are watching.

In the few weeks that Eddie (Michelangelo's most unforeseen fan) had been on campus, he had been watching me. In his life, paying attention to his surroundings was a simple matter of survival — literally. I was always outside with the kids (before and after school, between classes, at lunch, in the halls, and walking through classrooms) so he had seen me every day. I assure you he had quickly assessed me and formed a "battlefield" opinion of me.

2. Your kids are certain that they know how you will act.

Since Eddie had observed me so frequently interacting with other students, he had made some predictions about me. He couldn't help but do that, even if it was just a judgment that I was another guy in a coat and tie.

3. Your Kids are Certain That They Can Outsmart You.

When he arrived in my office that morning, Eddie had already decided that he wasn't going to divulge any information. He knew he could outsmart me by resisting my attempts to get him to cooperate and was thinking something like, "You're not going to get anything out of me, so I'm just going to shine you on" (politely so).

It was my understanding of these three things that ultimately allowed me to guide Eddie to cooperate with me. He predicted that I would assume him guilty and call the police. Instead, I tried to help him, and that must have been a rare occurrence in his life. I then disarmed him further by sharing art and beauty. He did not expect me to generously share something so obviously important to me. He thought he would easily outsmart me but he didn't predict I would change his emotion recipe by resetting his focus and physiology, so that I could connect with his emotional side and create a safe zone for him to drop his guard and become briefly vulnerable.

Let's look at how this same triad works in the minds of your own kids.

NAVY SEALS

I'm now going to reveal some Top Secret Kids' Information that has previously been classified "FOR KIDS' EYES ONLY".

You've heard of the elite Navy SEALs. You've seen them on TV and in the movies. The SEALs have a reputation for being highly effective at accomplishing their goals. A significant portion of their success can be attributed to the quality of their preparation, which involves loads of reconnaissance and observation.

Well, guess what? Your kids are Navy SEALs of reconnaissance and observation, too.

What does that mean? It means they're watching you. All the time. They are paying attention. And remembering.

Children of all ages are masters of surveillance. They have spent their entire lives instinctively studying the adults around them. They know what they can usually get away with, they know the best ways to get what they want, and they know how to push your buttons.

TOP SECRET (memorize this):
In most every situation where they interact with you, your kids have already internalized a predictable range of responses to expect from you.

Allow me to say that another way: because they've been watching you, your kids have cataloged an expected range of responses from you for every behavior that they exhibit. For each of the behaviors they exhibit, they know what to expect from Mom on a good day and what to expect from Mom on a bad day. Of course, the same applies to Dad, too. Your kids have been tracking your behavior more closely than Google or your credit card company. They are recording all this information and they know how to use it. They may not like what you say or do, but they are seldom surprised by your actions.

From your child's point of view:

➠ If I do this, then Mom will react this way, and Dad will react that way.
➠ I know which parent to ask to borrow money.
➠ I know which parent to ask to stay up later.
➠ I know which parent to approach first with a bad report card....

The important take-away here from a Navy SEAL "the-kids-are-watching" perspective is that we are often creatures of *unconscious* habit. It's easy for our behavior to slip into predictable patterns and habits — into auto-responses. And your kids are watching. **They especially remember the predictable things you do.** (This is often an "Aha!" moment for many of the parents I work with.)

Is that sinking in yet?

Now, I recognize that they are still kids and they often ignore what they already know and behave in ways that cause you to wonder, "WHAT in the world were you thinking?" **That's because they never really stop believing that they can outsmart you.** And that actually gives you great power! I'll show you why in a just a minute.

Ralph Waldo Emerson challenged all of us to be consistent with our actions and words when he wrote, "What you do speaks so loudly that I cannot hear what you say." Your kids are watching and remembering — even (maybe especially!) when you mess it up. But don't worry: in the Mindset section I'm going to equip you with some nuclear-powered relationship fixing and strengthening tools, including the PhD Apology.

Let's do another quick exercise that will drive this Navy SEAL concept home in a way that will allow you to forever see your actions differently.

TIC TAC RO-MEO

The exercise is waiting for you on the next page. When you turn the page (not yet) I want you to read each phrase out loud (you can whisper it if you want) and try not to think of the end of each phrase.

Okay, turn the page now.

Twinkle twinkle ...

Romeo and ...

99 bottles of beer on ...

Mary had a ...

Just do ...

May the force be ...

How did you do?

Even though you were trying not to think about the end of each phrase, it's almost impossible not to. These phrases have become embedded in our brains. Even when I try not to, I still hear "... little star" and "... Juliet" and "... the wall."

But it's not just silly phrases that become ingrained. Our behavior as human beings, and as parents, becomes automatic, too.

AUTO-RESPONSES

I recently ordered a copy of a friend's book from Amazon.com. I entered my credit card and shipping information and then as soon as I clicked the PURCHASE button, an email was sent to my inbox confirming my order. The response was automatic.

I sometimes discover that a friend of mine is on vacation with his family when I send an email to his work email address. A reply immediately shows up in my inbox with a subject line that says "OUT OF OFFICE RESPONSE". It happens automatically.

A software program sends both of these responses automatically. These emails are called, not surprisingly, auto-responses. They are pre-programmed and happen the same way every time.

Sometimes our behaviors look a bit like auto-responses. By doing or saying the same thing, the same way, day after day, a behavior becomes unintentionally programmed, automatic ... and predictable. And your kids are watching.

There are loads of predictable patterns of parenting behaviors. Think about how you ask your kids to do their chores or their homework, and how you respond when they ignore you and don't listen. Consider the "announcement scripts" you use to manage your children's chores. Do the words and tone of voice you use in these situations sound the same every day?

➠ Asking them to set the table
➠ Calling everyone to dinner
➠ Initiating the after-dinner routine
➠ Telling them to clean their rooms

There is great value in consistency. But pay attention to your outcome: if what you are doing now is not working, consider another approach.

➠ **ENGAGE:** Reflection Questions/Exercises (pdf)
In order for all of this to really sink in and create positive and lasting change I've created some short reflection questions and exercises for you to reflect on your parenting and to internalize these powerful new additions to your successful parenting repertoire.

Doing these exercises will strengthen your resetting techniques and mindset, and will give you the confidence to actually do this in the real world, with your real kids.

In case you feel like I'm pushing you a little hard, please understand I'm doing this out of my concern for you, your kids, and your grandkids. I want to be your biggest fan and I want to be your trusted advisor – and this is where as your coach I have to push you in case you're considering skipping this part

I've made it super easy for you by creating a Resetology Resources page where you can download all of the questions and exercises for each chapter.
http://www.resetology.com/book/downloads

RESETOLOGY BOOK CLUB
A quick-start guide for hosting your own Resetology book club.

PRESET
RESET
MINDSET

CHAPTER 4
Unexpected Resetters

RESET WITH THE UNEXPECTED

M Y FOUR-YEAR-OLD SON LEVI WAS PLAYING WITH HIS FRIEND MATthew when I heard yelling and crying coming from the room they were playing in. I walked in to find the boys on the bed fighting over a toy. Matthew was crying because Levi wouldn't share and Levi was yelling that he didn't *want* to share.

I'd already played referee several times and had spent way too much time trying to work out temporary solutions. So I decided to try a technique that Jim had shown me. I walked right up and asked,

"Would you eat a bowl of worms?" They stopped arguing immediately and started giggling. It was golden!

– Dr. Bob Uslander, ER physician

EMOTIONAL INTENSITY

All moods are not created equal. Some moods are positive (happy, excited) and some are negative (angry, frustrated). Intensity varies, too: emotional intensity can be low as in whining, or high as in raging. The majority of undesirable moods that you encounter with your children are low-intensity emotions. Your desired outcome in these situations is either to get them to do something (take out the trash, do their homework, practice their piano lessons, do the dishes, go to bed) or to stop doing something (stop bugging his little sister, stop whining or complaining, stop playing video games, stop ignoring you).

Dr. Bob wanted his young son and friend to stop fighting over the toy and play nicely. The first part of this chapter will prepare you to transform these types of low intensity emotions.

Okay, so it wasn't rocket science that Dr. Bob used to transform the boys' moods. But let's look inside his son's head for a moment at the three things (the triad) that are always going on.

1. He watched his dad

Levi watched his dad intervene several times, playing referee and creating temporary solutions.

2. He was certain he knew what to expect from his dad

His dad made several attempts to resolve the conflict, and Levi was certain that his dad would keep up the same repeated pattern.

3. He was certain that he could outsmart his dad

Levi was certain that he knew what his dad was going to do and that he could ignore his dad's continued efforts.

Succinctly put, the kids didn't expect Dr. Bob to surprise them. Then Dr. Bob did something unexpected, and the results were golden!

You can harness the power of the unexpected to transform your own child's undesirable moods. Unexpected things happen all around us. A door slams in the other room. You look up to see who it is, and when you return to your phone conversation, you can't remember what you were saying. If you were having an argument you may not even remember why you were angry. The slamming door was unexpected and your focus was reset.

Most parents already know that they can change a child's mood with a pleasant surprise, like an unexpected gift or party. It's amazing how fast a surprise trip to get milkshakes can improve grumpy or bored moods. Even just the anticipation of ice cream itself will snap most kids out of a funk, but the unexpected does not require big ice cream surprises.

Throughout the rest of the book I'm going to share some more examples of Unexpected Resetters in action, and I will mix in some stories from parents I've trained to show you how this works on the home front. After each story I share from here forward, I'm going to offer a little analysis of the Resetology™ elements at work. I'll point out the ingredients of the child's emotion recipe (focus and physiology) and the techniques used by me, or their parents, to reset their emotion recipe and transform their mood.

Let's continue with the dad with four boys we met in Chapter one.

KIDS' CHAUFFEUR BY DAY – AND BUSINESS EXEC BY DAY, TOO!

I had just finished chauffeuring my four boys back from practices, and was trying to finish up some work for a big, national client that I wanted to email before dinner. I had been prodding the older boys to do their pre-dinner chores when Mikey, my youngest decided that he had to go play at the neighbor's house – now. He was yelling insanely loud and ignoring my attempts to talk to him. I soon realized that I needed to do something different if I wanted to be able to finish my work, so I stepped away from the laptop and turned toward my son.

"Mike, Mike, hey Mikey," I said enthusiastically. Mikey stopped yelling and looked up at the sudden change in my tone.

"Let's try this," I said, waving him over next to me. "Stand up straight and put your arms out like this." Mikey stood next to me and imitated my movements.

"Good, Mikey. Now look up and smile at the ceiling. Good, now bounce on your toes." Mikey complied and began to laugh at the joy of sharing this silly moment with me.

"Am I doing it right, Dad?"

"You sure are, buddy!" I affirmed. "Good job!" Mikey beamed.

"Hey, why don't you go play cars in your room until dinner." I ruffled his hair as Mikey turned and raced towards his bedroom and the promise of great fun that awaited him with his cars.

And I was able to work uninterrupted for the next 20 minutes – just what I needed.

– *Robert,* **Dad of 4**

Here's a closer look.

Analysis of Unexpected Resetter

Robert's son was bored and the only way he could think to alleviate that boredom was to go play with his friend, now. Mikey had himself all worked up and was ignoring his dad's attempts to calm him down and change his behavior. So Robert unexpectedly invited his son into a new experience with Dad.

Focus

Robert got Mikey to focus on trying a fun new experience with his dad. By giving simple step-by-step instructions, Robert invited his son to concentrate on each new direction. His son was so engaged that he was focused on his technique.

Physiology

Robert quickly changed his son's physiology in many powerful ways. He got his son to:

➡ stand up straight and tall

➡ tip his head back and look up

➡ put his arms out in a manner normally associated with pretend flying (which tells his brain, "We're having fun!"), and

➡ bounce on his feet and smile

Robert had tried several times, unsuccessfully, to get his son to stop yelling. You've heard it said that the definition of insanity is doing something the same way over and over and expecting a different result. And yet, that seems to be a very common approach for many good parents. Does this sound familiar? First you tell your child to do something, and then if they don't do it you may give them a warning. Then you tell them louder and you keep raising your voice until they follow your directions. Finally, you regret the whole interaction.

But remember, your kids expect you to behave and respond in predictable auto-response ways. Herein lies your nuclear-powered strategic advantage: because they think they have you all figured out, it is remarkably easy for you to radically reset their focus or physiology — and hence their mood — simply by being ... unexpected. And there are thousands, nay, *millions* of ways you can respond to your children that will be unexpected!

Now that you are aware of some times in your life as a parent when you may act or respond to your children in the same predictable way, you can be strategically unexpected whenever you need to be. The more unexpected your behavior, the greater the impact it will likely have on resetting your child's mood.

If this seems a bit out of your reach, if you're thinking, "That may be easy for you, but I don't even have enough bandwidth to keep up with my kids as it is, let alone have the time to learn something new," please be encouraged. I'm going to make this easy for you and I'm going to walk you through this step by step. Here's a simple activity that will help drive this home.

IT'S NOT IN THE PICTURE

It's now time for me to reveal the depths of my God-given drawing skills. Take a look at this simple, inspired drawing I made of a tree and a simple house:

Does the picture look right to you? Is this picture complete?

On the lines provided below, write down three things that you do **not** see in this picture (and if you choose not to write them down, at least identify them in your mind).

1. _____

2. _____

3. _____

Well done. Now write down three more things that are not in the picture.

1. _____

2. _____

3. _____

Please try it before you read further.

Now I'd like you to compare your list to mine below:

⇒ sun
⇒ grass
⇒ birds
⇒ doorknob
⇒ windows
⇒ chimney

Does your list contain any of the items on my list?

My list contains the most common items parents write down in my live seminars. I've come to expect parents to include at least some of these items in their lists. Put another way, my list is a list of parents' predictable responses. And that's okay — almost everyone includes some of these predictable responses on their lists.

Now I want you to step outside of the predictable responses and write down three *unexpected* things that are not in the picture.

1. _____

2. _____

3. _____

Take a look at your list. How unexpected were your responses? Did you include anything wildly unpredictable? Maybe a microscope, or an elephant?

Imagine an elephant in the picture. Does an elephant seem unexpected to you? Well, let's make it even more unexpected.

Did you picture a normal gray elephant?

Let's make him blue with yellow stripes.

Does he walk like a normal elephant?

Nope — let's make him fly.

Is he normal-sized?

Let's make him poodle-sized.

And what is he doing?

How about playing a guitar and singing a Country and Western song?

We started with the rather unexpected image of an elephant standing next to our house and stick figure. But then we took the expected grey elephant of average size and transformed it into a puny blue-and-yellow-striped elephant that flies around strumming chords while belting out George Strait ballads.

Pretty unexpected, don't you think?

It's important to remember that **your kids view you in much the same way that you first viewed the picture of the stick figure and the house.** They think they have you figured out — as a stick figure.

And the beautiful thing is, just as there were an endless number of items *not* in the picture, there is also an endless number of unexpected ways you can reset your children's mood in any situation.

By examining how you interact with your children, and becoming aware of your predictable patterns of behavior, you will discover your auto-responses and how your kids expect you to act in any situation.

Then, any response that is different from what the child has come to expect will be surprising and unexpected. Their surprise will reset their focus, which will reset their emotion recipe, guiding them to a more positive emotion.

Change the ingredient ⫸ Change the emotion recipe

Change the emotion recipe ⫸ Change the emotion (mood)

Remember, you're already one of those amazing parents who is seeking more tools to help you do the hardest job on earth. That fact alone makes you remarkable. Now let me show you how to take the amazing power of the unexpected and supercharge it!

Clarification

Before we go further, let me make one important clarification regarding consistency. You may be thinking, "I thought it was important to be consistent and predictable as a parent." And you would be right. Consistency is one of the most important elements of an effective parenting plan. You need to have a parenting plan and you need to work that plan. That is not what I am addressing here. I am referring to those situations where "what you know" isn't working. And remember, every parent I've ever worked with — every GOOD parent like you I've ever worked with — confesses that they have plenty of frustrating repetitive interactions with their children, situations where their normal parenting stuff doesn't work.

Sometimes the wheels fall off. For those times when you want a different outcome — a different mood or behavior for your child — Resetology™ will prove indispensible.

➡ ENGAGE:

Practice with a Partner – Five Easy Steps to Resetting (pdf)

In order to make it easy for you to practice with your partner, I've created a simplified practice guide for you with the *Five Easy Steps to Resetting*. I have also included a couple of additional tips not found here in the book.

Access it at: http://www.resetology.com/book/downloads

CHAPTER 5
Dramatic Resetters

RESET WITH A TOUCH OF THE DRAMATIC

DON'T WORRY: I'M NOT GOING TO ASK YOU TO MEMORIZE ANY LINES OR GET up on stage. Dramatic resetting is simply the unexpected on steroids! It's a super-quick shortcut to the unexpected. You don't even have to change the words you normally say to your kids — just how your voice sounds or how your face looks.

While being unexpected is generally achieved by saying something surprising, being dramatic is achieved through a surprising delivery of message.

Unexpected = Surprising Message

Dramatic = Surprising or Theatrical Delivery of the Message

If this sounds like a stretch for you, let me remind you of how you may already have incorporated the dramatic in your own life. Think about how your behavior changes when you are in close proximity to a baby. What happens to your face? Your voice? Your vocabulary? Expressions and silly voices emerge that are seldom seen in any other situation. "Did I really just say 'blanky-wanky'? Is that baby-frog voice really coming from me?"

We intuitively know that if we want to connect with a baby, we need to change our normal demeanor. And that demeanor change is a touch of the dramatic. If you have ever made goo-goo eyes or cooed to a baby, then dramatic resetting will be a piece of cake for you!

Have you ever seen a stoic older man who generally doesn't show much emotion, light up around his little grandkids? He becomes like a little kid himself. When he tries to get a baby to smile his face suddenly fills with an impressive array of ridiculous smiles, pouts and expressions. Where did that come from?

How about when that same grandfather, with his usually limited range of facial and vocal expression, reads a picture book to his grandchild? Almost magically, a broad range of theatrical expressions and animated voices appears. He even reads the story out loud with different voices for each of the story's characters — and his energetic reading captivates the young listener!

But babies aren't the only ones who respond to dramatic variations in typical behavior. Any exaggerated look upon your face or animated inflection in your voice will instantly be perceived as different and unexpected, and it can change any child's focus and reset their mood.

Let me illustrate this with a bedtime story from Thom, a dad who attended one of my seminars.

My daughter had just finished her shower, brushed her teeth, and – well, it should have been time for stories, then bed. But she didn't want stories. She wanted to watch more television, and specifically more cartoons. She was beginning to get really angry when I said no and explained that it was already too late and that it was time for bed, and we were not going to be watching any more television.

"I'm not going to sleep until I get to watch another show," she said.

"You're not watching more television tonight, and you are going to sleep right now, and if you keep this up you won't get a story either!" I declared. She persisted, but this time with angry eyebrows, a growl, and even a few small threats.

I thought it was time for some Dramatic Resetology™.

I stuck my neck out as far as I could, opened my eyes as wide as possible and stared at her eyes with laser beams. The contortions must have made *me* look like a cartoon.

"What are you doing?" she asked.

"I'm winning," I said.

"Winning what?" she replied.

"The staring contest. The first person to laugh loses," I said.

Almost instantly she started staring back. It lasted for about 10 seconds before she exploded with laughter.

"I think I just won," I said. "One more time?"

We played again, and then a third time, all within a minute.

Now she was laughing a bit, and the growling had ended. I sat next to her and gave her a hug and said, "Thanks for playing with me. I had fun with you today. We can watch some cartoons tomorrow, but right now we're all tired, and it's time to go to bed. Which story do you want me to read?"

She picked a story and the rest is history.

Many of the parents I've trained confess that bedtime is a source of much frustration.

Thom was able to reset this frustrating situation with a simple use of the dramatic.

Analysis of Dramatic Resetting

Thom made exaggerated facial expressions – the kind of expression that kids are used to seeing in cartoons. Kids are wired for entertainment, so anything that whiffs of entertainment will capture their focus.

When she found out it was a contest, his daughter immediately engaged in it by staring back at him.

Focus

The child's focus reset instantly because she was trying to figure out what crazy thing her dad was doing.

He turned the interaction into a fun contest.

Physiology

Thom's daughter held her eyes wide open and resisted her natural inclination to blink. Laughing helped, too.

Warning

You should know that there are some risks associated with Resetology™ — Dramatic Resetology™ in particular. When using Dramatic Resetology™ you are at risk of creating wonderful lifelong memories; strengthening relationships; and connecting more deeply and frequently than ever before.

What's the worst danger associated with using Resetology™? You are also at risk of embarrassment — in the eyes of your children. But that's not such a bad worst-case scenario. In fact, your *willingness* to show your kids a fun, goofy, silly side of you will yield many powerful life-long benefits for your kids.

You model some important life lessons:

- It's okay to take risks.
- It's okay not to be perfect.
- Embarrassing yourself is not a big deal, so they should never let fear of embarrassment prevent them from pursuing their goals.
- It's okay not to take yourself too seriously.

You strengthen your connections with them:

- Through crazy moments, you can create powerful bonding because your embarrassment removes your ego from the playing field.
- You share a ridiculous memory that you may treasure and laugh about forever.
- You radically increase the balance in your kid's Positive Relationship Savings Account (learn more about this in Chapter 8).

Think of the risks that you have chosen to take in your personal life, with your business, or with your finances. Regardless of how they turned out, it is very unlikely that they yielded anywhere near the positive return on investment that risking embarrassment in front of your children will yield. (Note: I said embarrass yourself, *not* them. More on this distinction in the "Having fun *with* vs. Making fun *of*" section in Chapter 11.)

And if being goofy in front of your kids yields so many positive benefits for your kids, why would you worry about it? It's really all about your willingness to have fun and be silly at times.

If you are concerned that your touch of the dramatic is not Broadway-worthy, fear not, because this can actually work in your favor. If your kids think your effort at being dramatic is ridiculous, it will be all the more effective at resetting them.

Here are a couple of stories from the principal's office where I use the dramatic to reset students' moods.

"All-roit then – stop!" I said with the butchered English accent of a guy who never took drama class. The third grader's eyes got big, his mouth spit out a few more words until it caught up with his brain, and then he stopped. He was fervently trying to convince me that his teacher should not have bought him to my office.

"Oy want to 'ear everything you 'ave to say," I continued, "but you 'ave to tell me in an Eeenglish awk-cent. Cawn you speak in an Eeenglish awk-cent?"

"Hu – huh?" Jeff stammered through his confusion.

"Oy said you 'ave to tawk in an Eeenglish awk-cent."

"I can't," Jeff deflected.

"You mean, Ah-ee cawnt," I corrected. "Go awn, give it a troy."

"Mrs. Baker said that I have to stay in at recess to finish my homework."

"You mean, Mz Baker said oy 'ave to stay een ta feenish me 'omewuk," I countered.

He started to speak normally one last time, and I shot my hand up to stop him. He stopped. I raised my eyebrows in expectation and rolled my hand over, gesturing that it was his turn.

Jeff took a deep breath and started again: "She said oy have to stay in to finish me 'omework," he managed, then exploded into a face-stretching grin. Game over. Three minutes later he calmly left the office, agreeing with the reasons that he had to spend his recess time working in the office for a few days.

Let's look closer at the Resetology™ elements here.

Analysis of Dramatic Resetting

Jeff certainly wasn't expecting his principal to speak in a foreign-sounding voice. The dramatic always has a sense of performance to it that makes people take notice.

I wasn't smiling, so he knew I was serious, but he was radically confused by the accent I was speaking with.

Focus

First Jeff was just confused. Then when he realized that I expected him to imitate me, he had to listen carefully to try to understand exactly what was different about how I was talking, so that he could attempt it himself.

Then he had to focus on speaking with an accent he had never used before.

Physiology

Jeff had to experiment with his voice to try to create the sounds of an English accent.

We've seen that even simple Dramatic Resetters can quickly transform a child's undesirable mood; however, the full-blown theatrical stuff can yield amazing results, too. Here is one middle-school lunchtime scene that I'll never forget ...

I opened the office door and walked into a chaotic din of disobedience. Fifteen middle-school kids, their veins coursing with a potent cocktail of early-adolescent hormones, had been sent to the office by a lunch supervisor. It was like a scene out of an out-of-control teen movie where the students overrun the school cafeteria. They were yelling, taunting, and standing on chairs. Outnumbered, my talented but beleaguered secretary was vainly trying to restore order.

I realized instantly that I could not yell loud enough to be heard over the cacophony, and I needed to capture everyone's attention quickly. I had to do something different. So instead of yelling, I started singing an old Nat King Cole song:

Maybe the sun gave me the power,
For I could swim Loch Lomond
And be home in half an hour.

Everyone froze. Voices stopped mid-word. All eyes turned to me.

I stopped singing, stood tall, and waited. I held the silence. (The look of relief and gratitude on my secretary's face was priceless.) Immediately the students started shrinking back to their assigned seats. When all were seated, I quietly stated my expectations for their waiting-to-see-the-vice-principal behavior. I also told them the consequence for breaching this expectation. I then had them all stand up, and then sit down, to acknowledge that they had understood my directions. They remained quiet and respectful thereafter while I quickly dealt with them in small groups in my office.

Most of these kids had never been sent to the office before, and they got caught up in the mob mentality. However, some of the kids really were misbehaving. It was a perfect storm of misbehavior, and it sounded as though a bunch of cats and coyotes were were dying loudly to the accompaniment of claws on a chalkboard.

Analysis of Dramatic Resetting

I started singing! Singing is entertainment and entertainment is fun, so it was immediately detected by the students' fun radars. Just as music soothes the savage beast, the singing pierced right through the noise and drained all the energy out of the situation.

Focus.

Their focus went immediately from "This is crazy, new, and wild!" to "Oh crap, I'm busted. What was I thinking?"

Physiology.

The singing caused all the first-timers in the office to freeze, and the office frequent fliers were just a step behind them. So, whatever their physiology was doing before – moving fast, talking loudly and rapidly – all of those physiological elements vanished in an instant. Then they slowly walked to their seats and sat quietly.

I got them further invested in my expectations for their behavior by having them all stand up.

Now it's time for you to get started with Resetology™!

FIVE EASY STEPS TO RESETTING SUCCESS

Congratulations on making it this far. Your commitment is inspiring! Now it's time to try Resetology™ for yourself. I'm going to make it easy for you, so let's jump right in!

1. Get a Resetting Partner!

Make this as easy as possible right from the start and invite someone to join you! Your chances of immediate success will go way up if you find a practice partner. It can be anyone. A friend who also has kids, a friend who doesn't have kids, a neighbor you like, your spouse, a co-worker. A partner will provide you with support, encouragement, the opportunity to become a skilled resetter, and accountability.

2. Select a Resetter

Browse through The Vault (a collection of Resetter Cheat Sheets) at the back of the book and find a Resetter that you would like to try first.

Some of the Resetters™ are very subtle, like pointing out the apparent softness of the stone in Michelangelo's *Pieta*. Others are more like a getting a glass of cold water in the face. I'll show you both kinds. And just for the record, while an unexpected glass of cold water in the face will certainly reset someone, there are very few instances where you would actually use that. So try to match the appropriate Resetter with the situation and with the child.

Even though I have created and used over 100 different Resetters, I have found that there is a handful that I use most frequently. As a principal, I used these "go to" Resetters with probably 50 percent of the kids I dealt with. You may find the same is true.

3. Read the Cheat Sheet

Read the directions for the Resetter a couple of times, until you feel comfortable. While you read, try to visualize yourself using the Resetter.

4. Practice, Practice, Practice

I encourage you to practice each Resetter a few times before you use it. You can make this fun by using a little role-play with your resetting partner. Have some fun with it. Practice being silly and unpredictable: it will make it easier when you use the Resetter with your kids. Laugh at each other. Encourage each other and give each other suggestions. Challenge each other to make it even more unexpected or dramatic.

If you do not have a partner, I recommend that you practice in front of a mirror: the mirror won't laugh at you, so you'll have to laugh at yourself. Surprise yourself! By practicing each Resetter, you'll feel confident that you know what to do when the opportunity arises. Here's a hint: your Resetter does not have to be word-for-word from the Cheat Sheet to be effective.

Another benefit of rehearsing in front of the mirror is that you can practice using different faces and poses. These are not essential, but can add a significant impact to your Dramatic Resetting!

Pre-load the Resetter. This is a simple step of mentally preparing yourself to reset. And give yourself a personal locker-room style pep talk:

➡ Have fun
➡ Be confident
➡ Be surprising
➡ Be expectant
➡ Be flexible
➡ Be compassionate
➡ Be ready for some amazing results!

Prepare yourself for action by reviewing the Get-Set Checklist in Chapter 7 and becoming familiar with it.

5. Try it out!

Don't wait until you can do this perfectly — start right now! You don't have to wait for an emotionally volatile situation to try Resetology™ for the first time. Try a Resetter in a random situation *just to see how your child reacts.*

Go try it right now. Walk up to one of your kids, hold out your hand as if you were offering them a bowl of candy, put a curious look on your face, and then ask them, "Would you eat a bowl of worms for a hundred dollars?"

➡ ENGAGE: Share Your Stories – Help other parents

I would like to invite you to share your own stories of resetting with your fellow parents. There are some important reasons to consider doing this:

YOU can help other parents and kids. Other parents may identify with your specific situations in a way they did not connect with my examples. The light bulb may go on for them, and they suddenly see how or when they can use Resetology™ in their own life. Not only does this have the power to help the parents, but their kids benefit as well.

These can be videos or you can write them out.

Submit stores/videos at http://www.resetology.com/share-your-story

CHAPTER 6

The Dimmer Switch

HOW TO QUICKLY CALM

W E'VE LOOKED AT HOW TO USE THE UNEXPECTED AND THE DRAMATIC TO transform undesirable moods of low intensity. But what do you do in those red-zone situations when you've had a exhausting, week, tempers are flaring, your child is being a serious pain, and you're worried you might say something you would regret for the rest of your life?

Buckle up. I'm about to teach you the exact same technique I used to quickly calm big, raging teens who had just minutes before been in serious fist fights. Prepare to equip yourself with the calming power of the Dimmer Switch!

Air Jordans

An over-sized eighth grader stormed through my door a step ahead of his security escort. A lunchtime conflict had landed him in my office. Marc dropped aggressively into the open chair and white-knuckled the armrests in defiance.

"I didn't do it!" he yelled with the added volume that middle-schoolers often think will add credibility to their story. I reached for my pad to take notes.

"Tell me what happened," I said.

"I didn't do it," Marc shouted again, and launched into his story. Soon enough he got louder and louder and started slapping the arm rests. I stopped writing, leaned forward, and stared intently at his shoes. He kept shouting his angry story for a few seconds, while I slowly widened my eyes as if in amazement.

"Those are really cool shoes," I said enthusiastically.

"Wha —" he said, as his eyebrows scrunched in a "what-are-you-talking-about" look. But when he looked down at his shoes and back at me, I knew that I had hit pay dirt. When he looked up, I said, "I'm sorry, tell me what happened."

Marc restarted his story. I took more notes until his volume began to rise then I reset him again.

"Do you wanna trade?" I said as I wheeled my chair around and put my Cole Haan loafers near his expensive Air Jordans. "They're about the same size."

He started to grin, not completely sure that I hadn't lost my mind.

"Sorry, tell me again what happened," I said as I wheeled back in front of him.

Then he calmly told me the story until, at one point, his volume began to rise again. So I said, "Are you sure you don't want to trade?"

Marc instantly smiled, recovered, and finished the story. He was transformed from furious to calm in just two minutes, and was now politely discussing the situation and the consequences of his actions. It was a complete victory for both of us.

HIGH-INTENSITY EMOTIONS

Have you ever thought, "I'm gonna lose it!" or "I'll show you who's boss!"

One parent told me, "I don't want to be that parent who yells, 'Just get in the f***ing car!' to his kids. Because we all know that parent."

Here are some comments that are representative of the responses I get from parents when I ask them to finish to finish the sentence, "I feel out of control when…."

➡ When I am bombarded with a million different things all at once.
➡ When I boil over.
➡ When I lose my temper.
➡ When I don't want to do the things that my dad did, that I hated.

Parents often tell me that they feel powerless to deal with situations when their child's emotional intensity is high, because they have exhausted their parenting techniques, and they don't know what else to do.

It's now time to learn about the quick-calming power of the Dimmer Switch! So successful was the Dimmer Switch in calming irate students that my secretaries would often invite others to observe the rapid calming through my office window.

THE DIMMER SWITCH

When I was a kid, I used to play with the dimmer switch that controlled the lights in our dining room. I was pretending to cut off the power in the secret spy lab that I was sneaking into. I would turn the lights all the way up to maximum brightness, and then slowly turn the dial back the other way so that the lights would grow dimmer and dimmer until all the light had faded.

The "Dimmer Switch" is the term I now use to describe the specialized process of repeatedly using a Resetter to calm a child quickly. Using Resetters in the manner explained below has the same effect on the intensity of emotions as turning down the dimmer switch has on the brightness of a light. As you reset repeatedly, the intensity of the emotion dims and fades away.

You have already seen the calming power of the Dimmer Switch in the story about the irate boy and his Air Jordan basketball shoes at the beginning of this chapter. So now let's prepare you to get the same results with your own children. For some of you, it will seem as though you've discovered fire all over again.

How To Use the Dimmer Switch

First of all, you want to make sure that you are in the best possible emotional state to reset. There's a detailed framework (The Get-Set Checklist) at the end of this chapter that will guide you through that process.

Here's the magical sequence for resetting with the Dimmer Switch:

First Reset

1. Get the upset child's attention and engage them (e.g. ask the child to tell you why they are so upset; make eye contact and listen to them – be sincere).
2. Reset them when their emotion becomes intense.
3. Apologize.
4. Encourage them to continue.

Second Reset

1. Allow their emotion to resume intensity.
2. Reset them a second time.
3. Apologize.
4. Encourage them to continue.

Third Reset

1. Allow their emotion to resume intensity.
2. Reset them a third time.
3. Apologize.
4. Encourage them to continue.

You can repeat again if necessary.

You can do this — it's not complicated. Here is another visual representation of the Dimmer Switch process in action:

This simple process is repeated until the intensity of the emotion (represented here by the size of the type) is dimmed and the child is calm. Depending on the situation, you may only need to reset one time to calm the child. You will be amazed how this simple process magically dims the intensity of the child's emotion each time you reset with a Resetter.

Let's go back and see how this method applies to the Air Jordan situation, walking through it step by step.

- First, I allowed Marc's emotional expression to become intense before I reset him.
- I then reset him, three times, focusing on his shoes.
- After I reset him, I apologized and encouraged him to continue his story, which allowed him to re-generate emotional intensity. (I find that the apology helps maintain my connection with the child throughout the process.)

Now let's take a closer look.

Analysis Of the Dimmer Switch

Unexpected

- This irate young man did not expect me to make a fuss over his expensive basketball shoes.

Focus

- Marc's focus was first changed when I said, "Hey, those are really cool shoes!" and my face exploded into a smile.
- The second time I reset his focus was when I wheeled around and put my dress shoe next to his Air Jordan and asked, "Do you wannna trade?"
- And the final time was when I asked him again, "Are you sure you don't want to trade?"

Physiology

- There was a radical morphing going on in Marc's face. The first time was when his angry face scrunched into the "What are you talking about, you crazy weird principal" look.
- Then there was a secondary morphing when he realized, "Oops, maybe I shouldn't give the principal a 'you're weird' kind of look."
- He then had to intentionally steer his focus back to the angry situation when I encouraged him to do so.

Now, let's go even deeper and look at some other important elements of the Dimmer Switch that will amplify its effectiveness for you.

I showed interest

➡ I communicated to Marc that I was interested in his story and that I cared about what he had to say when I took a pen out and started taking notes.

➡ I read it back to him to see if I had captured the story correctly. That was another quick way for me to affirm that what he was saying had value.

➡ I also had my chair facing directly at him.

I apologized

➡ I find that quickly apologizing after each reset helps to maintain our rapport. The quick apology gently bridges us back together because I honestly want to be present to the child. I want them to know that I am still listening and that they are being heard.

I paid attention

➡ Before he landed in my office for fighting I already knew that Marc's shoes were important to him. I had observed that he had many pairs of expensive basketball shoes. He wore a super clean pair for each day of the week. His shoes were more expensive than mine!

Here's another example of the Dimmer Switch in action.

A Bowl Of Worms

The police delivered Jerry to my office at 10:00 a.m. Jerry was a scarecrow thin, goofy-looking seventh grader who honestly believed that people viewed him as a tough guy. To the rest of the world he looked like a middle-school nerd with an incongruous attitude. He had been picked up truant at a nearby mall. Jerry knew that he had earned an automatic after-school detention, which meant that he would miss after-school basketball — his favorite thing in the world. So he stood before me with that condemned-man syndrome: since he had already lost basketball, he felt he had nothing left to lose.

Still, Jerry had done nothing wrong while at school, and I had to get him into class. But he was clearly not disposed to cooperate in a classroom. Chances were very good that if I delivered him directly to his class, he would instantly do something to get kicked out. In fact, I probably wouldn't make it very far back down the hall before the classroom door would open and from behind it I would hear the teacher holler: "Mr. House, will you please come back here!"

It gets worse. In Jerry's mind, the only thing worse than being escorted out of a classroom by an assistant principal was being escorted *into* a classroom by an assistant principal. Jerry's middle-school sensibilities had him terrified of being escorted into class. If I could calm him down, I could escort him to his classroom door and let him walk in by himself with dignity. But he was angry and frustrated and determined to get me to take him, instead, to the in-school suspension room.

Observe how I used the Dimmer Switch on him.

We join the conversation as Jerry is trying to convince me that he shouldn't go into his class because the teacher is singling him out.

"He's a jerk!" Jerry spouted, with arms crossed tightly across his chest. "That guy hates me! He shouldn't even be a teacher if he doesn't like kids. He picks on me and never calls on anyone else. No one else has to —"

I held my hand up to him as though I were offering him a bowl of candy, and with a curious look on my face I reset him, "Would you eat a bowl of worms for a hundred dollars?"

He jerked his head back and sported a don't-mess-with-me face.

"No!" he snapped, his face reflecting a rebellious sense of triumph.

"I'm sorry. So he only calls on you?" I asked, and he launched back into his anti-teacher tirade. When the volume peaked, I held my imaginary bowl up to him again and proposed, "How about ten thousand dollars? Would you eat a bowl of worms for ten thousand dollars?"

"No way," he said unconvincingly, as his arms uncrossed and his whole body relaxed deeper into the chair.

"I'm sorry, you were talking about your teacher." I put a concerned look on my face and waited for him to continue.

He paused, not sure what to say, and then, "Yeah, that guy doesn't like me," he said, only mildly irritated.

He stopped briefly as if trying to understand where his temper had gone, and then forced himself to continue, "If I don't have my homework he — "

"What about a million dollars?" I chimed in excitedly, holding my hand out again. "OH MY GOSH! Do you know what you could buy with a million dollars?" Jerry laughed out loud.

"I don't know," he said sheepishly, and we began planning how we were going to get him back into class successfully. It worked.

How did that happen? Were you able to follow how I used the Dimmer Switch with Jerry? Let's walk through it step by step.

- ➡ First, I allowed his emotional expression to become intense before I reset him.
- ➡ I then reset him, three times, with Resetters — in this case, with the Dimmer Switch Resetter "Bowl of Worms".
- ➡ I apologized each time I reset him and encouraged him to continue his story, which allowed Jerry to regenerate emotional intensity while maintaining my connection with him.

Did you notice how his *physiology* softened each time I reset him? His physiology transformed from "arms crossed tightly" to "laughing out loud".

And each time I reset him, his *focus* was diverted from desperately trying to stay out of his class to trying to comprehend my ridiculous bowl-of-worms offer.

As a result, his emotional intensity quickly diminished and he went from angry and afraid to confused and sheepish — in about a minute. He made it successfully into his class and the rest of his day went well.

➡ **ENGAGE:** Dimmer Switch graphic (pdf)

Download an easy-to-read graphic showing the simple steps of the dimmer switch for you in two sizes: fridge-sized and wallet-sized. The wallet-sized version has the Get-Set Checklist on the back, so you have the resources you need wherever you are.

http://www.resetology.com/book/downloads

CHAPTER 7
Pre-Flight and Maintenance

GET-SET CHECKLIST

BEFORE ANY PILOT TAKES OFF IN ANY KIND OF AIRCRAFT, SHE RUNS THROUGH a pre-flight checklist. The checklist ensures that everyone onboard will have a safe and successful flight.

The Get-Set Checklist we're going to talk about in this chapter works just like the pilot's pre-flight checklist — but instead of taking off you are taking stock of a situation. The Get-Set Checklist is a simple six-step inventory that you run through to make sure you are prepared to reset.

The first three checklist items are designed to ensure that you are not part of the problem. These steps will help you to show up calm, alert, and able to access your best decision making for the situation. After trying it out, one parent confessed to me, "To be completely candid, it also is teaching me to take a step back before reacting or, worse, overreacting. I find that I can often be as much a part of the problem as anyone."

It will definitely be worth your while to become familiar with the checklist. The checklist is quite intuitive, so you may only need to review it a couple of times before committing it to memory, and it will rapidly become second nature.

GET-SET CHECKLIST
A = AWARE
B = BREATHE
C = CALM
D = DECIDE
E = EXPECT
F = FLEXIBLE

A = AWARE

Be aware of safety first. Safety is always the most important factor and is worth dwelling upon. Sometimes resetting is not the right option. Sometimes you may just need to appropriately stop a child from doing something that could harm them or someone else, or damage property.

Become aware of the physical environment. Make a quick risk-analysis assessment. Are there any potentially dangerous elements? Streets or cars? Heights? Curbs? Any breakable items? Is it a public place?

Become aware of the whole situation. View the scene as a wide shot in a movie that encompasses all of the important variables, not as a close-up that focuses on only one person's face. Be aware of who is around you in addition to your child: their friends, your friends, relatives, coaches, strangers, etc. The consequences and damage done by embarrassing your child in front of others *may* be catastrophic. So, just be aware of who else is nearby.

Then exercise your **prudent comprehensive parenting judgment** to determine if this is the right time to reset. You have to be the judge of that. And in order to be the best judge, you have to be at your best — in a high-functioning mood and state of mind. So become aware of your own emotional state: your own focus and physiology. When we are upset, our field of vision narrows and we can't access as many options (it's the flush of stress hormones that does this to us). So you need to consciously override your physiology. Which leads us to Breathe.

B = BREATHE

Breathing is the grandest Resetter for all of us. Radically impacting the rate and volume of oxygen going in and out of our lungs leads to rapid mood transformation. It's powerful stuff.

Here's how you take control of your own physiology: take some purposeful breaths. This kind of breathing prepares us physiologically, neurologically, and emotionally to deal with a situation in the best possible way that will get the best possible outcome.

Here are two ways to impact your emotional state through breathing:

---

1. Nose breath cadence (beginners)

➡ Breathe in through your nose for a slow count of five.

➡ Hold for a count of five.

➡ Exhale through your mouth for a count of five.

➡ Hold for a count of five.

➡ Repeat.

2. Underwater-swim breaths (advanced)

➡ Try filling your lungs with as much refreshing, new oxygen as you can, as though you were about to swim a lap of the pool under water.

➡ Hold for a count of five.

➡ Exhale explosively, as though you were trying to blow out a candle five feet away.

➡ Hold for a count of five.

➡ Repeat.

(Note: while it might be funny to watch, for safety reasons hyperventilating is not recommended as a Resetter.)

C = CALM

You can always choose your emotion, and it's really important to choose calm. (Again, if safety is a factor, do what needs to get done to ensure safety first.) Take deeper, slower breaths in through your nose. Talk slower. Speak softer. Make slower movements. Be confident and calm. Pretend you are trying to fill the space around you with your calmness. Calm is powerful.

No matter how crazy a situation was in the schools where I worked, I always kept my calm. When the campus was in lockdown because a gunman ran across the playground, my staff looked to me. Because I was calm, it gave them permission and confidence to be calm as well.

Seldom do you gain anything from being angry or having an outburst. Admittedly, there are times when a sense of urgency in your voice can be helpful and even necessary. But my advice is to go there only on purpose — never accidentally, in reaction, or by default. Don't let your temper rule you. Decide when it is beneficial to raise your voice a bit, and then do it purposefully and in complete control.

You set the tone. If you are erupting or overreacting, your kids will gladly accept your invitation to do the same. Kids are always looking to you in any situation — they will notice your response and often will take their cue from you. Remember, they are Navy SEALs of observation.

If your emotional intensity is ramping up, theirs will escalate, too. They will climb the ladder of voice volume and intensity with you, rung for rung. When you choose calm, it becomes more difficult for them to keep advancing up the emotional intensity ladder and sustain craziness. The discrepancy between their intensity and your reaction becomes more apparent, and they have to generate all that negative energy by themselves. This is more difficult for them to sustain.

More importantly, when you are calm you retain your full faculties and maximum access to all of your strategic tantrum-busting Resetters and other parenting strategies. Which leads us to Decide.

D = DECIDE

You are aware of the situation. You have taken some good, purposeful breaths to help you maintain a positive and productive emotional state. You have chosen calm to set the tone for the interaction. And now you are ready to **decide** which Resetter to use.

What is the intensity level of the child's emotion? Do they need to calm down? Or are they just bored or grumpy?

Review the selection of Resetter Cheat Sheets provided in the Vault at the back of this book, or refer to one of our other Resetter resources at Resetology.com. (I have created over 100 proven Resetters.)

Sometimes you will decide to be unexpected. Sometimes you will decide to be dramatic. Sometimes you will decide to be dramatically unexpected. The needs of the situation will determine whether you are resetting to:

➡ transform an undesirable mood

➡ quickly calm, or

➡ just connect

You have to decide which Resetter to use. Does the situation call for the subtlety of a gnat flying at the edge of a child's peripheral vision, or the sudden impact of a glass of ice water in the face?

Some Resetters work best with one child; others can be used with small or large groups. Some Resetters work better with younger kids, while others can be used with the oldest of teens. Some Resetters work in any situation. But don't worry: if your focus is securely on helping the child, you can't mess this up — especially if you are fully present.

You can always step out of the room, open this book to the Vault section, quickly scan a Resetter Cheat Sheet, and then return to reset. This is how some of you will operate. Others will prepare several in advance. Do what works for you. Once you've decided upon a Resetter, it's time to reset!

E = EXPECT

When using a Resetter, it's important that you expect it to work. If you think it will work, it will work. If you think it won't, it won't. That's because we broadcast our level of confidence, and a child will know if you have doubts about using whatever you've got up your sleeve.

If you approach resetting tentatively, like the freshman boy at a high school dance who approaches a girl and says, "You don't want to dance with me, do you?" it will be less effective. But rest assured: given the impact of the unexpected, even if you do execute a Resetter tentatively, you still may get the outcome you desire simply because it *is* unexpected.

Remember, you are not trying some experimental technique here. Be confident in the knowledge that I have used Resetology™ successfully with literally thousands of kids, of all ages, in all sorts of crazy situations, *and* loads of parents have already gotten the results you desire with your own kids.

Also, enjoy the realization that you are not *re*acting. You are using a positive, proactive method. That's great! Congratulate yourself! Believe it is going to work and have fun with it!

F = FLEXIBLE

Resetting always works, but your expectations may be off. Sometimes it works bigger and better than you expected, and sometimes it works more subtly and covertly than you expected. So stay flexible. Read the impact of your resetting — like a professional sports coach assessing the last play before deciding which play to call next — and then make your next move. The big change, really, is that you are in control: you are acting, directing and coaching, so stay flexible and don't get flustered.

There are not many new skills that you can acquire and immediately apply with perfect success. While Resetology™ may be the exception to that rule, the reality is that the reason I created over 100 Resetters is because some of them just didn't work the way I wanted them to with certain kids, so I invented new ones. There was definitely a handful of Resetters that were my go-to Resetters, and I used them frequently. Always be willing to try a different Resetter. Maybe the first one you tried wasn't the best Resetter for the current situation, so be open to trying it again at a later date.

THE LAW OF FAMILIARITY (OR FAMILY-ARITY)

Think of a song you liked from some period of your life. When you first heard it on the radio, you thought it was catchy and you enjoyed it. But after you heard that song played every hour for days, and then weeks, the novelty eventually wore off. Unless you had a special memory attached to the song, it became too familiar to engage you, and you were on to the next new song. Familiarity rendered that song lifeless.

There is no scientific law of familiarity that I am aware of. But it sounds like there should be. Doesn't it make sense that when something becomes familiar, you pay less attention to it? When it becomes familiar, it becomes predictable. Families, especially parents, are predisposed to succumbing to predictable behavior patterns, so I call this phenomenon "family-arity".

Think of some technique that you used in the past to reward or motivate your child to complete their homework or do their chores: maybe it was stickers on a chart, or extra playtime. Perhaps it worked well for a while, but did it wane in effectiveness over time? Did it eventually lose its ability to motivate your child? That's one of the dangers of familiarity — it sucks the power out of things. The same thing can happen to Resetters. No matter how effective they are, they may eventually become predictable and lose their power. Take a look at how I handled this situation with Angela.

"Mr. House, you think you know everything! ... Mr. House, you think you know everything! ... Mr. House ..." she chanted in a loud, looping mantra. Angela was a very large and intimidating eighth grader. She stood almost tall enough to look me in the eyes, and everyone on campus gave her and her sour disposition a wide berth. Angela had been sent to my office after a lunchtime confrontation.

A "Discipline Frequent Flier," Angela was no stranger in the office. We usually had productive conversations after she calmed down, and she was making noticeable progress with her social skills. But this time she was determined to stay mad and resist any calming techniques by chanting that phrase over and over – like a small child shouting "nah nah nah nah" and plugging their ears to communicate, "I'm not listening!"

"Mr. House, you think you know everything!" Angela continued with fervor. So I stood up, walked away from my high-backed chair, and gestured for her to sit down in my chair.

"OK, let's switch – now you're the vice principal," I said. Her loud chanting stopped, her mouth froze open, and her eyebrows lifted high. She wasn't completely convinced that I was serious. I just stood there, patiently pointing to the chair.

Angela got up slowly and approached my chair with the kind of reverence usually reserved for thrones, or the seat next to Oprah. Angela lowered herself into the chair and immediately assumed a stately posture.

"Now pretend that I'm you – I'm the one in trouble," I said. "How would you handle this situation?" She promptly gave "me" an appropriate consequence and counseled me as to how I could have avoided the conflict. She even asked me questions in the same way that I usually did.

When we switched seats again, she was fully aware of what had transpired and gracefully accepted the appropriate consequence, which she had prescribed for herself. It wasn't magic, it was science.

Like Angela in the beginning of this story, your children can become desensitized to the impact of a specific Resetter. But don't worry: I have a special plan for preventing this. I call it the Resetter Rotation.

RESETTER ROTATION

This is the scheduled maintenance portion of Resetology™. We have already learned how effective Resetters are at defeating predictability. However, each Resetter™ has a half-life of unexpectedness. Even the most successful of Resetters™, if used repeatedly, will eventually become familiar and then lose its effectiveness.

With the Resetter Rotation you are in a constant cycle of acquiring, using, and retiring Resetters. The rate of acquiring and retiring Resetters will depend on how often you use a particular Resetter and with whom you use it. Here's a simple way to approach your Resetter™ Rotation. At any given time, there are three Resetters™ in your Resetter Rotation:

One Resetter coming online (learning or installing a new Resetter)

One Resetter online (Resetter you are using or ready to use)

One Resetter phasing out (retiring Resetter: phasing out, perhaps to resurface in the future)

The Resetter Rotation works great! But even if you are not prepared, and your rotation isn't yet fully planned, you can always wing it — that's the beauty of Resetters. Or you can step out of the room for a minute, open up this book to the Vault, quickly scan a Cheat Sheet, and then return to spontaneously reset!

➡ **ENGAGE:** Get-set Checklist
Download and print your own copy of the Get-Set Checklist™ to hang on your fridge as reminder for yourself (and even your whole family)!
http://www.resetology.com/book/downloads

CHAPTER 8

Connect

We've forgotten that we belong to each other.
— Mother Theresa

How are you?
Busy. You?
Really busy.
— Conversation overheard ... everywhere.

B USYNESS SEEMS TO BE A BADGE OF HONOR THESE DAYS. I, TOO, FIND MYSELF saying, "I'm really busy!" when someone asks how I am. Much of that busyness is created by the vast number of ways that we interact with people: email, texting, Facebook, Twitter, and the rest. It's an unfortunate paradox of our world today: we are digitally linked together in so many ways, but how often do we truly connect with other people — especially our kids?

Interaction does not necessarily imply connection. Even face-to-face interaction does not necessarily lead to real connection. Yet we all long for connection. We all want to be understood, and accepted, and appreciated, and seen — truly seen. This may seem obvious, but there is massive value in connecting with our kids. **And know this: even if you don't see it by their actions, your kids crave connection with you.**

Connection provides a protective umbrella of esteem under which your kids can grow and develop. It gives your child wings and helps them to develop into the best possible version of themselves.

There are also benefits for you. Connection provides a solid foundation for you to be able to approach your child and deal with issues together. It also makes you accessible and puts you on the same team. You can face issues and deal with problems better from a shared position than you can from an adversarial position.

Connection is really about getting out of the way to reveal what is already there — what has always been there. If connecting is new to you, this is going to be a huge and reassuring revelation. Connection begins with a one-way decision and action — your action.

There *is* a clear path to deeper and stronger connection with your kids, but first I want to introduce you to an important metaphor that we are going to use for the rest of this book:

The Positive Relationship Savings Account.

Imagine that you have a Positive Relationship Savings Account (or PRSA) for each of your children. Just like the savings accounts you have with your bank, you can make both deposits and withdrawals. But the interesting thing about this savings account is that the only accepted currency is not money, or toys, or anything material. This account only accepts deposits of love and connection. Every single positive interaction with your child will deposit a little bit of currency into the account and increase the balance. However, the big six-figure deposits come in the form of real connection. That's what really makes this account grow.

The balance in this account is dynamic: it's either going up or it's going down. It's never static. Your interactions are always impacting the balance.

Picture that Positive Relationship Savings Account for each of your children. How often do your interactions with each child make deposits? How about withdrawals? Fill them up with positivity every chance you get. You can't create love and connection without making time for it, and the rewards of connection go only to those willing to invest.

It is important to note that the balance of the PRSA rises whenever your actions benefit the growth and well-being of your child. It does not necessarily mean that your actions should make your kids smile and like you as a person in every moment. Sometimes great parenting, and love, demands that you make decisions that anger your children. That requires courage, and those difficult moments can dramatically add to the balance of the account, even though it may not become apparent for a long time.

The rest of this book is going to help you connect with your children on a deeper level.

You will remember that Resetology™ is made up of three components. In the **Preset** section of this book you learned that all emotion recipes are comprised of two ingredients: focus and physiology. In the **Reset** section you learned how to transform undesirable emotions and quickly calm kids with Unexpected, Dramatic, and Dimmer Switch Resetters. In the final section, the **Mindset**, I am going to show you a unique four-stage process for building strong connections with your kids.

I believe this is so important that the rest of the book will be dedicated to maximizing your Parenting Mindset.

Let's get started!

PRESET
RESET
MINDSET

CHAPTER 9
Time Travel to the Present

WELCOME TO THE MINDSET SECTION AND CONGRATULATIONS FOR COMING this far!

Now, I do have some God-given talent for connecting with kids, but beyond that, I've paid very close attention to the precise conditions that strengthen connections. I've made the study of connection my life's work. The strategies contained within each stage of the Mindset have been developed and refined over more than 25 years of quickly connecting with thousands of kids in all sorts of situations. I did not invent all of these strategies; I've just been hyper-vigilant about noticing what works with kids and then applying those principles.

Over the next few chapters you will learn the strategies, habits, and techniques that will help you to fill your children's Positive Relationship Savings Account to overflowing. I am going to guide you through the four stages involved in building strong relationship connections with your kids: **Time Travel, Not So Fast, What You Really Long For, and Repair and Restore.**

TIME TRAVEL TO THE PRESENT

The first stage in developing the Resetology™ Mindset is preparing to connect with your child in relationship. Stage One contains four habits:

➡ Be Present
➡ Be the Calm
➡ Love (probably not what you think)
➡ Pray (this job is too big to do alone)

This stage focuses on the habits that will help you prepare yourself to approach and engage your children in deeper connection. This is about getting yourself ready first — before you interact with your child.

Be Present

The first relationship habit is the art of being intentionally in the present moment — the now. I apply this habit in my life every day and enjoy being continuously amazed at how it transforms the ordinary into the extraordinary, how it improves me, and how it unlocks the potential of those I touch. In the long run, this will be your most important relationship investment strategy.

I am going to show you how to recognize little distinctions that will help you become present and remain present. It's like the tricks of the trade a coach shows a player, or a friend shows a cherished companion. Once I point out the distinctions, you're going to be amazed that you didn't see them on your own and amazed at how they pop up everywhere, inviting you to fine tune what you already do well and make it great!

You can go "there" any time, even all the time, and it's the only place where the magic can happen. Just where is this enchanted, elusive place? Well, it's technically not a "where," it's a "when." And the when is now. The present.

While the present is of course a time, I've found it helpful to think of it as a place: a special place where relationship magic happens. That makes it easier for me to guide you there.

So how do you get to the present? Time travel!

I love to travel and the first thing I do after I decide upon a new travel destination is to go buy a guide book that will tell me what I need to know. I've created a special travel guidebook to help you on this journey. Like all good travel guidebooks, we'll cover your destination, getting there, and what to see and do. I call it...

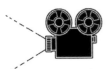 

The Resetology™
Time Traveler's Guide
To The Present

YOUR DESTINATION

You have probably heard about "being present." It is a concept frequently used in psychology, spirituality, and personal development. The present has many names: the Now, the Present Moment, and even the Sacrament of the Present Moment. It means that your focus is completely here, in this moment. Presence is just pure you.

Let's look at a timeline to help make this clear. There are only three places your thoughts and focus can be:

| Thoughts of the past | The present | Thoughts of the future |

There's the past: stuff that has already happened to you. It's really easy to focus on the past and reawaken negative emotions like regret—especially as parents.

There's the future: stuff that I think will happen someday. It's easy to live here, too.

And then there is the present—the now—which is where I want you to reside. In the present you are not thinking about the past or thinking about the future.

Most adults spend most of their time focusing on the past and on the future, completely missing the present:

| Stuff that has already happened | Stuff that hasn't happened yet |

Even with the best of intentions, good people still spend lots of time focusing on the past and the future. But when we are in the company—I'll say the *sacred* company to highlight how precious a place this is—of a child, we owe it to them to be present in the moment with them.

The present

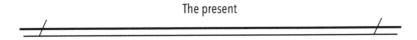

This is where the relationship investment gold is found. This is the magical place where you want to reside.

So What Does the Present Look Like?

Imagine yourself looking at your child through a camera's viewfinder where the depth of field has blurred everything except your child into irrelevance. Distractions magically disappear as you arrive at the here and now. I find that any anxiousness I may be experiencing instantly dissolves. You may see time slowing down a bit, and you will definitely see your child in a richer way.

Where Is the Present?

The present is always available wherever we are. We just need to travel to the now.

The present is wherever you and your child are together: sitting on the couch, walking the dog, eating at Subway, or washing the dishes.

Make no mistake: I'm not saying that you lose yourself in some naive bliss that ignores the requirements of daily family life. Being present is more about who you are while fulfilling those requirements.

What Are The Benefits of Being In the Present?

The more you are able to walk through your child's life being present, the more your Positive Relationship Savings Account balance is going to overflow. You will notice your kids—really notice them—and you will know how and when to interact. That may sound fuzzy, but you have to trust this. Even if you don't say any words to your child, I assure you they will know that you are being present to them, and that knowledge will pour lots of love onto them.

GETTING THERE

Since the present is a time, not a place, getting there requires a specialized mode of transportation.

We all know that time travel requires a time machine. Well, I have hooked us up with a remarkable time machine. This is not the garden-variety Jules Verne-style time machine you've seen in science fiction movies. Those machines all seem to look like a steampunked version of Santa's sleigh. Ours looks very different. Two huge movie screens on opposite walls dominate the interior of our time machine. Flanking my seat in the middle of the craft are two noisy old-fashioned movie projectors that are constantly projecting movies onto the screens in front of and behind me.

You will not be surprised to learn that the first part of time travel is physiology and the second part is focus.

Pre-flight: Physiology

Here's the physiology pre-flight routine I go through before I board the time machine:

1. Breathe in deeply through your nose. Pay attention to your breathing: notice the flow of air.
2. Notice your entire body. Feel the chair, your feet on the ground, and the clothes against your skin.
3. Hear the sounds. Become aware of all of the ambient sounds surrounding you.

After you do this a few times, it may only take a few seconds. Once you have checked in with your physiology, you are ready for time travel. Four easy steps will take you where you want to go.

Pre-flight: Focus

Step One: Turn Off the Rear-Screen Movie of Thoughts of the Past. Picture yourself sitting down in the cockpit of the time travel machine. Remember, there are movies playing on huge screens in front of you and behind you.

Swivel your seat to look at the screen behind you. The rear movie projector is showing scenes from your past, flying across the screen with whirring speed:

* scenes of regret
* why did I do that?
* I should have
* if only I had done that differently
* you should have seen me when I was your age

You don't want to spend any time watching that movie and focusing on the past, so in your mind, reach over to the projector and flip the power switch OFF. There's a loud clunk as the reels stop and the rear screen goes dark.

Step Two: Turn Off the Front-Screen Movie of Thoughts of the Future. Swivel your chair 180 degrees to look at the screen in front of you. The front projector is flashing scenes from your future:

* scenes of excitement, fear, worry, concern, hope, anxiety ...
* who's going to drive you to practice tomorrow?
* I need to get dinner started
* I should answer that email tonight
* how am I ever going to finish this?

You don't want to spend any time watching this movie either, so reach over to the projector and flip the power switch OFF. There's a loud clunk as the reels stop and the front screen goes dark.

Step Three: Arrive. Once both screens go dark, the whole time machine instantly evaporates and vanishes, and a quiet calm rushes in. You look around and find yourself smack dab in the middle of where you are – and the present is unveiled. Suddenly, you find yourself in an amazingly peaceful, unhurried, positive place – alive! It's as though someone has turned on the lights to reveal where you always were, but could not see. I'd like to officially welcome you to the present!

Step Four: See The Child. Be *with* your child – not just near. Get eye contact. Remind yourself that it's not about you. Remind yourself that your child is a miraculous creation, and that you are privileged to be in their presence. Remember, too, that they are just as lucky to be with you!

Here's the Resetology™ time travel procedure in brief:

Pre-flight: Physiology

1. Breathe in deeply through your nose
2. Notice your entire body
3. Hear the sounds
4. Pay attention to your breathing

Pre-flight: Focus (quiet the noise)

1. Turn off the rear-screen movie showing thoughts of the past
2. Turn off the front-screen movie showing thoughts of the future
3. Arrive. Remind yourself that you are just a person sitting/standing/walking – you're not your resumé or your agenda
4. See your child. Notice your child. Be with your child.

WHAT TO SEE AND DO

Welcome to the present! You are one of the few who actually reach this remarkable destination. It's surprisingly rich here, isn't it?

All good travel guidebooks make recommendations about which sights to see in each new place, and provide practical advice for getting around and interacting with the locals. Similarly, this section of *the Resetology™ Time Traveler's Guide* will provide you with practical suggestions to help you make your stay in the present as long and as meaningful as possible.

Okay, you've found your way here to the present, but it's not easy to remain here. Because many of us spend so much time focusing on the past and future, it is easy to accidentally "eject" ourselves out of the present: like accidentally pushing the ejector seat button in one of James Bond's Aston Martins. I'm going to show you what these buttons look like, so you can avoid them. I'm also going to share a couple of powerful Presence Resetters (amplifiers) that I sometimes use when I'm especially distracted and struggling to remain in the present with a child. Again, it will not surprise you that I have organized these tips by focus and physiology. Let's begin with focus.

Eject Buttons

Once you arrive in the present, those pesky thoughts of the past and the future still try to muscle their way back into your focus. Even when your intention is to just be with a child, these types of thoughts—the eject buttons—will ambush you and throw you out of the present. These are some of the most common eject buttons that you will be tempted to press while inside the present moment:

* thinking about what you're going to say
* thinking about how we are going to fix this
* worrying about what they will say
* worrying about what you are going to do
* worrying about consequences
* worrying about what they will think about you
* wanting them to like you

When left to their own devices, our brains naturally generate endless streams of thoughts like these. Do you ever find yourself thinking any of these sorts of thoughts when trying to be present with your child?

Trust Yourself In the Present

You'll have to learn to trust that you will have something to say and not try to manipulate the outcome of the conversation. What experience has abundantly taught me is that when I intentionally shelve my agenda, the right thing to say always appears when it's my turn to talk. In fact, better responses show up when I do this. It was really difficult for me at first to trust and allow this to happen.

I can speak with far too much authority on this matter because it's so easy for me to focus on what I'm going say next, instead of listening when someone is talking to me. It's an unexpected fruit.

Another surprising and humbling observation I've discovered through being truly present to someone talking to me is that I frequently have nothing to say when they finish talking, I have nothing to add. And I am certain that no response is the best response in those situations. I am embarrassed to say that in most conversations I had prior to learning this, I forced words into a space where just silence and presence was required.

Train Yourself To Trust and Hold the Silence

Silence can feel painfully awkward and excruciatingly long: a mere 10 seconds can seem like forever. But sometimes silence is precisely what is needed to coax meaningful disclosures, thoughts or questions from your child. These are thoughts your child may never express if you rush to fill the awkward silence with your own words that do not originate from a place of presence. Trust the silence and trust the present. You will know what to say and when to say it. Of course, there may be times that you honestly don't know what to say. I can assure you that being consciously present with a child during times like these will be far more beneficial to both of you than if you were to force some words into the silence.

While it can be useful to prepare in advance for a critical conversation you need to have with your child, you won't need to memorize your words if you show up in presence.

Presence Resetters

Some time ago, I read that there are two very different ways you can enter a room filled with people. You can enter and say, "Here I am!" or you can enter and say, "There you are!" Well, there are also two ways you can enter an interaction. You can approach the child with the attitude of "Here I am!", which puts all of the focus on you. Or, you can approach the child and say, "Oh, there *you* are!", which puts all of the focus on them.

That deliberate focus on the other person amplifies my ability to remain present and resist the eject buttons. These presence amplifiers keep me humble and keep me focused on what is truly important.

So how do I keep the invading thoughts of past and future from ejecting me out of the present? Here are the two Presence Resetters I told you about.

I had the privilege of participating in a four-day ministry inside a maximum-security prison, and this ministry (run by Kairos) had a powerful motto for all of the "outside guys" who worked the weekend. I have integrated that motto into my life and it is my first Presence Resetter:

Listen. Listen. Love. Love.

Saying this simple phrase inside your head is a powerful way to remain present. Don't think about your agendas. Don't worry about impressing your child with your "I've-got-it-all-together" parenting skills.

As soon as the time machine vanishes and I find myself in the present, the first thing I say to myself is: Listen. Listen. Love. Love.

That reminds me that this interaction is not about me. Then, when I notice myself thinking about my agendas (eject buttons), I gently remind myself to: Listen. Listen. Love. Love.

I say these words silently out loud in my head: Listen. Listen. Love. Love. Honestly. Try it. **Listen. Listen. Love. Love.**

Please say it again. **Listen. Listen. Love. Love.**

And again. **Listen. Listen. Love. Love.**

The reason I dared to lead you into that blatant sequence of repetition is because this is gold! Lock these words into your brain. Use these words as a reminder to help you stay present during the sacred interactions with your children.

But what about those situations when you just don't want to be present? There are times when I just don't feel like being present. I can be so preoccupied with my own agenda that I resent someone else trying to catch my attention. I want to shout, "Not now! Just give me a couple of minutes!" I might just be in a funk doing something insignificant, like trying to see the instant replay of an amazing catch or get that last load into the dryer. Or I might be at a critical point in an important task like crafting an important email.

I find the second Presence Resetter especially beneficial during those times when I'm likely to view an interruption as an intrusion into my own productivity, instead of as a chance for loving interaction.

I borrowed the words for this Presence Resetter from the Christian Scriptures, where John the Baptist is talking about Jesus right at the beginning of his ministry. I apply them to myself when I need to rip my ego agenda out of my head and focus on a child:

Increase you. Decrease me.
Increase you. Decrease me.

The words call me to immediate humility, and I say them over and over in my head until I can become present. They are powerful by themselves and they become amplified when I attach them to my breathing:

Breathe in: **Increase you.**

Breathe out: **Decrease me.**

This Resetter also helps me time travel to the present in order to be present to a child.

Be a Participant, Not a Director

Be a participant in the conversation – not a director. You may guide the conversation, but from *inside* of the conversation, not the outside.

Be open to hearing what your child says and don't be so quick to fix or comment. When they are talking to you, enter into their story. Leave your own story behind and enter their world. Hear everything they are saying, uninterrupted, without stopping them. You are selflessly "sacrificing" your agenda to gift them with your complete presence. It is the purest of gifts. Kids know when you are engaged and they respond differently: they are engaged too. Remember, they are Navy SEALs of observation and reconnaissance. You can't fool them here.

Of course there will be a time to think, and plan, and perhaps teach, or give consequences, but begin with listening. And trust that being present will help you to access the best possible response. This is not easy to do, but it's incredibly worthwhile.

We need to be present to hear ourselves, as well.

Here's a life hint: these methods will deepen every interaction you have. If you listen to people like this, you will be rewarded with a richness in your life that will seem remarkable.

Be Affirming

You've heard the famous adage that every critical statement we say to a child needs to be balanced out with ten supportive statements. I do not know the research behind this ratio, but I think we all know from our own experience that our own Positive Relationship Savings Account rises when the affirming statements we receive from someone greatly outnumber the critical ones. And the more the better.

As humans we remember and own our negative experiences more easily than we remember and own our positive experiences, so I encourage you to *err on the side of over-affirming*. At *every* moment, kids are inherently worthy of being told that they are loved, and are worthy of lots of other affirmations too.

There's a popular sentiment these days that kids should only be praised when they earn it. People who support this sentiment point out that kids now receive trophies just for participating, even when they come in last place. In the minds of many parenting experts, the remedy to this is to praise kids only when they earn it. I respectfully disagree. There certainly is value in validating specific behaviors to increase their likelihood of repetition. There is value in "catching" a child doing something good. But this presupposes that the child has to do something worthy of praise in order to receive praise. Unfortunately, sometimes kids are most in need of praise precisely during those times when their behavior is far from praiseworthy. I understand the notion of "love the child, correct the behavior"; but all too often, what I witness comes across as conditional love.

Try to be present when you affirm: don't just sling nice words at your children. Kind words and affirmation offered in presence seep deeply into a child's soul because they know that you truly mean them. And by the way, the words "I love you" have staggering impact when spoken from a place of presence. The same is true of any affirmation. The state of the person doing the affirming can be more important than the actual words of affirmation.

There was once an outraged student in my office who would not respond to my attempts at resetting his emotional state. I intuitively knew that what this student needed in this specific moment was some sort of affirmation. The problem was, I couldn't find anything about him to affirm: his behavior was deplorable, he was making absolutely no progress in calming down, and his clothes were filthy. So, while being present to him I infused the following statement with as much sense of importance as I could muster, and I complimented him: "Nice breathing."

His rage switch clicked off and he was instantly calm. Even I didn't expect it to work that well. The reason I share this story is that while this student wasn't exhibiting any praiseworthy behaviors, what he needed most in that specific moment was praise – affirmation. Now, breathing is clearly not a praiseworthy behavior (you can't be a bad breather), so the affirmation was the critical element in transforming his state.

Physiology: What's a Body Got To Do With It?

It's not just your focus that time travels to the present; your body goes, too. In the Time Travel Pre-Flight routine, you already grounded yourself physically by noticing your breathing, your body, and the ambient sounds around you. As soon as I turn off the past and future movie projectors, I further ground myself physically in the present by looking at my surroundings and saying, "I am here."

There are three additional physiological strategies that will help you maximize your time in the present.

Develop Facial Expression Awareness.

Your face betrays more about you than most people realize. A massive percentage of the message you communicate through body language emanates from your face, so it is in your best interest to develop what I call "facial expression awareness." Learn exactly what message your face is sending at all times. Start checking in with a mirror frequently to become aware of what your face really looks like at different times—and more importantly, to discover if your face really looks like what you think it looks like. What feels like a calm, neutral expression to you may look like frustration to the rest of the world, for instance. Here's a story that one of the dads I trained shared with me:

> *"Are you mad at me, Daddy?" asked my six-year-old daughter. Her words jolted me out of my analytical trance.*
>
> *"No, baby, no. Daddy's just thinking."*
>
> *"I'm glad you're not mad, because you look mad."*
>
> *"Thanks, honey, come here!" I recovered as I scooped her up into a big daddy bear hug. "How are you doing, my Wendie?"*
>
> *I run six businesses and my mind never shuts off. Unfortunately, my unconscious thinking face is sometimes a grumpy-looking one. D***, I'm working on that.*

Steal a peek at the mirror (or take a "selfie" with your phone) during different moods, especially right after an interaction with your child, and discover what your face is really saying.

Use Hips To Be Square

When you are interacting with your child, try to face them straight on as much as possible. Maximize the amount of your physiology aimed at them by aiming your face, shoulders, and hips directly at them (when appropriate, of course--don't do this while driving a car!). This communicates very clearly to the child that you have just made them the most important thing in your life in that moment. I learned this trick from a British soccer coach when I was in middle school. He said that if you watch the ball handler's feet, they can fool you. But if you watch their hips, the hips will tell you exactly which way they are really committed to go with the ball. The same principle holds true with attention. It works because the hips and shoulders broadcast unmistakably where your focus is committed.

Turn Away From the TV!

Don't just turn your head to talk to your child when they approach you. Turn away from the TV and square your shoulders and hips toward your child. Turn away from the TV, turn away from the dishwasher, turn away from the laptop, turn away from the barbeque, and turn toward your child and toward connection. Welcome interruptions with your physiology.

Of course, you are not going allow them to be rude by interrupting an important activity or another conversation, but when it is time to give them your attention, give them your full attention.

I am not suggesting that children should have instant access to you: boundaries and limit setting are critical components of effective parenting. However, I encourage you to develop awareness of your own physiology during both welcome and unwelcome interruptions.

> The better you become at being present to yourself, the better you will become at being present to your children.

This is the end of *The Resetology™ Time Traveler's Guide To The Present*. However, there are still three additional habits that will help you prepare yourself to Connect: Be the Calm, Love (probably not what you think) and Pray (this job is too big to do alone).

 Thank you for Time Traveling with us. We hope you return to the Present real soon! (Please come back often!)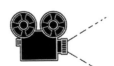

BE THE CALM

Ghandi once said, "Be the change you want to see in the world." So, with all respect to the great man, I'm going to paraphrase him and say, **"Be the calm you want to see in your child."** It starts with you. Remember that calm is the third step in the Get-Set Checklist (Aware, Breathe, Calm . . .). This is so important that I have also included it as part of the Resetology™ Mindset.

Calm is power.

There is great power in remaining calm, especially in stressful situations. I don't mean manipulative or aggressive power, but rather the kind of power that allows you to:

➥ access and make your best decisions
➥ set the tone for an interaction
➥ give your kids permission to de-escalate their emotions

Remember, your kids are watching all of the time. If you're calm, they're noticing that you're calm, or at least they're noticing that you're not yelling. And they recognize that you are not engaging them in a power struggle (a battle of wills).

Here's a note I received from an attorney I trained:

> Dear Jim:
> I can't possibly overstate how helpful and effective your Resetology™ is. Not only has it helped tremendously in defusing situations and overcoming conflict with my children, but it also has proven to be an effective method for me to deal with conflict and difficult situations in all aspects of my life, so long as I remember to use it. To be completely candid, it also is teaching me to take a step back before reacting or, worse, overreacting. I find that I can often be as much a part of the problem as anyone. I strongly endorse the technique and believe it has great potential for use in a broad fashion to bring peace in the midst of conflict.
> – *Maria*, Attorney, Mom of 3

There are two beliefs that help keep me grounded and calm in all situations:

> **Belief #1:** No one's bleeding, no one's dying – we can handle it.
> **Belief #2:** There is a solution to this.

BELIEF #1: NO ONE'S BLEEDING, NO ONE'S DYING – WE CAN HANDLE IT

I stole this motto from a physician friend of mine, and I frequently said it out loud to myself and to others when a situation became stressful at school. Now, there were many times when people were actually bleeding, and we had quite a few ambulance visits, but in most circumstances it proved to be a potent perspective Resetter — a "30,000-foot view" of the bigger picture to help ascertain the relative gravity of a situation.

At school, crazy stuff happened more regularly than you would imagine.

Armed Suspect On the Playground

I was walking up to the office when one of the secretaries came running out of the door in near panic. She told me the police had called to say an armed-robbery suspect was approaching our campus and he had a gun. I intentionally spoke slowly and quietly as I told her to return to the office and sound the alarm bell for lockdown. She took a deep breath and then quickly carried out her duties with a new sense of calm.

All the doors on campus were immediately locked, all students and all adults went to the nearest building, and teachers had their students get under desks and away from the windows. This procedure was well rehearsed.

Fortunately, no classes were outside. I did a quick sweep of the campus and as soon as I was certain that everyone was inside, I called the police for an update. By that time, they had the suspect in custody a few blocks away, and the school day returned to normal.

Dead Body In the Field

No one said it out loud, but as my office staff leaned in closer, I could see it in their eyes: "Did you really just say there's a dead body across the street?" Two minutes prior I had glanced out of the office window and had indeed seen a dead body lying in the field across the street from the school with officers standing nearby. In 45 minutes, the dismissal bell was scheduled to ring and 1,300 middle school students would pour out of the school, many of whom would walk right past the body on their way home.

But if the body was still there when the bell rang, we were going to have to hold those 1,300 sixth, seventh, and eighth graders inside their classrooms.

So I had called the office staff together, told them what was going on, and given them quick directions. My voice and demeanor were ultra calm. With lightning speed, we needed to put plans in motion to notify teachers, parents, bus drivers, and the district office, and prepare to execute a host of other items. The huge demands of these contingency tasks were enough to inflict serious stress upon the already busy staff. And there was still a dead body across the street.

But they knew their tasks and, more importantly, they knew that I wasn't freaked out. Assured that everything was going to be fine, they set to their tasks with aplomb.

I was pretty certain that there weren't any safety concerns because none of the officers over there in the field was moving with any sense of urgency. Of course, I had to find that out for sure first. I went across the street to talk with the officers and they assured me that there were no safety issues. Having established this, I did want to see a little more speed happening, so I explained to them that if the situation was not resolved within 30 minutes, I was going to have to postpone dismissal. I explained what that would look like: there would be loads of concerned and angry parents; I would have to write a letter home; bus schedules would be impacted throughout the entire district; and the newsworthiness of this story would rapidly escalate with the appearance of a school lockdown and a fatality. The officers instantly understood the implications and pulled off a miracle. Ten minutes before dismissal, the field across the street was once again vacant. When the bell rang the students never knew any different.

BELIEF #2: THERE IS A SOLUTION

I'll never forget the morning of my first day of school as principal. Teachers were just leading their students in from the playground when several staff members came running to inform me that two parents were having a loud and volatile screaming match in front of the school. Parents arriving late to drop their kids off were freaking out, so I collected the two women and brought them into my office. As soon as I closed my door their high-volume exchange resumed. I had no idea how I was going to resolve this shout fest, but I was calm because I believed that there was a solution.

We emerged 20 minutes later and found the entire non-teaching staff in the front office, all pretending to be busy. They were shocked when we emerged calm and civil. I think they were all standing near a phone and, in their heads, practicing dialing 911.

In each of these three situations, I remained calm and projected calm even when I didn't know what to do. I share these stories simply to highlight the value of remaining calm, even in the most intense and dire circumstances. I could have made any of these situations much worse if I had gotten agitated and barked orders. Hopefully you won't have to deal with armed robbers, corpses, or near parental fisticuffs, but you certainly will have frustrating situations where calm seems just as elusive.

As a good parent, you know that kids actually (and silently) crave boundaries. Well, the same thing applies when they are in a full-blown emotional storm. They often want to get off, to stop the tantrum, but they don't know how. They want you to be calm — to be an anchor stuck firmly to the bottom of the ocean that will only let them stray so far in their storm.

LOVE

You already know about love. Here's the critical part of love as it relates to the Resetology™ Mindset:

> The more you love yourself, the more you'll be able to love your kids.

Here's a litmus test I learned for loving yourself: if you can look at yourself in a mirror and say, "I love you," to yourself without feeling uncomfortable, you are doing okay.

Make no mistake: this is not an original idea of mine. Some time back, a great man said, "Love your neighbor *as yourself.*" This is worth some thought.

Being the best parent you can be in all situations is excruciatingly challenging. In my opinion, there is no opus, no legacy you could strive for that is more meaningful and valuable than being the best parent you can be in all situations. You cannot do that without lots of love for yourself, too.

I want to offer one simple Perspective Resetter regarding love from a mentor of mine that can be useful to remember: You can be right, or you can be loving, but not always both.

PRAY

I would be doing you a huge disservice if I did not include this critical piece of my Mindset. Turning to prayer is one of my favorite personal Resetters. Prayer is what gives me all of this stuff. When I'm having difficulty being present and I become aware that I need to transform my thinking from "Here I am" to "There *you* are", prayer is my secret shortcut.

Let me share a quick story about how prayer has influenced this book. I've been a serious goal setter for my whole career. Every year I would go to a hotel out of town for a weekend to reflect on the previous year, and to set goals for the coming year. I would take along a cassette tape or CD of a Tony Robbins goal-setting session that I would play over and over. I spent two days in that hotel room in a peak emotional state, visualizing the outcomes I wanted to achieve in the coming year, identifying the actions I needed to take, and then packing them with enough purposes and "whys" to make sure they happened. It was a very effective system. I set goals in all categories of my life, but I always picked my top three goals for the year to home in on.

While prayer has always been essential to who I am, for many years I was reluctant to focus on my prayer life as one of my top three goals. I didn't want to "waste" one of those coveted top three spots on a goal that I thought I should be working on every day, in any case.

Three years ago, I finally decided to make prayer one of those top three goals. I chose to spend about an hour a day in prayer and quiet meditation. It was during that year that Resetology™ really took off. A coincidence? Definitely not. This book and my ability to help parents and families flourished when I made prayer time my most important priority of each day.

I offer this to you just to remind you that some priorities are more important than others in achieving what's most important to you.

And pray for your kids. It's like making stealth deposits into their Positive Relationship Saving Accounts!

➡ ENGAGE: Time Travel pdf

I've created a quick-reference guide containing the steps for Time Traveling to the Present. You can download this and carry it in your wallet or purse!

After you've mastered the steps you can use it as a reminder be present – something we all can use!

http://www.resetology.com/book/downloads

CHAPTER 10
Not So Fast

THE SECOND STAGE IN DEVELOPING THE RESETOLOGY™ MINDSET IS APPROACH-ing to connect with your child. There are four elements:

- ➥ remove your sandals
- ➥ all kids are good
- ➥ respect
- ➥ be an actor, not a reactor

REMOVE YOUR SANDALS

As a parent, you probably spend much of your day in task mode, solving problems and getting the stuff of life done. Most of the daily interactions with your child fall into this category of "getting life done." But you can intentionally step outside of the normal daily life stuff and into connection with your child. You probably already do this quite a bit; here's another path to deeper connection with your child.

There is a great image in the Hebrew Scriptures where Moses removes his sandals to acknowledge and remind himself that he is treading on holy ground. This simple act is a powerful gesture of reverence and humility. What if you were to imbue a similar sense of reverence into some interactions with your child?

I invite you to approach your child with the awareness that you are entering sacred space. You already know that your child is precious beyond value, otherwise you wouldn't be reading this book. But it's easy to take for granted. So, gently remove the shoes from your "task-mode mindset" and approach your child with reverence, with the expectation that something truly remarkable is about to take place. And know that every minute is a gift — it's all gift.

Focus completely on the child and become curious about what fruits these moments may yield. If you want to connect, you need to make your child the most important thing in your life at that moment. You may cook dinner for your family each night, but every now and then you choose to make a special dinner to honor someone. Approach some of your interactions with the same sense of specialness.

Many busy parents only realize this deep sacred truth in hindsight; don't let that be you.

A Resetter for Parents

Consider trying this Resetter to remind yourself that you are stepping out of your own world and stepping into a sacred time with your child. Remove your shoes — gently, don't just kick them off. Sit down and slowly take each shoe off and carefully lay them side-by-side on the floor. Take a couple of deeper breaths. You can try this in calm situations, or in situations where you may need to compose yourself.

Equal Worth

Here's another reminder that may help you slip out of your ego shoes. They may be two feet shorter than you and a whole lot younger than you, but your child's inherent value as a human being is equal to yours. You have the same worth. However, you do not have the same roles and responsibilities. It can be helpful to remember that this child, who at this moment may be acting like a major pain, is no less a miracle than you are.

Don't Assume Rapport

Connection can only be granted to you — you can never take it. Sometimes you need to "knock" on the door of connection with your child before moving forward. Be aware that you may not be in the same "relationship place" you were in the last time you connected. I would never discourage you from engaging or hugging your child; just retain the awareness that they are an autonomous person who may not be on the exact same page as you. Don't dwell on this: just let it exist as an awareness.

Kids always notice when you stop and connect with them using these techniques. When you engage your child with an unexpected Resetter, they know that you could have interacted the way that you usually do — your auto-response. They know that you are choosing to interact and engage with them; that you are taking time to notice them, to acknowledge them, and to be with them. Your kids know you have a busy life, but when you decide to interact with a child, you are saying very clearly that they are the single most important thing in your life in that moment. This is amplified when the interaction is fun.

Seeing Eye to Eye

Just before the teachers left for summer every year, I asked them to fill out a simple anonymous evaluation of me. My first year as a principal one of the teachers made me aware of a behavior that I was doing automatically when I spoke to kids. She responded to the "I'd like you to do more of ..." prompt by writing this:

> *I love how you get down to their eye level whenever you speak to a child on the playground or in a classroom.*

So here's the physiology tip: when appropriate and possible, get down to a child's eye level when you listen to them and when you talk to them. This posture goes a long way toward honoring the child, making them feel "seen" and communicating that you value them, which strengthens the connection.

Of course, many interactions between parent and child are just operations-related, the conversations that make everyday life happen (schedules, carpools, homework, meals, laundry, chores). Even so, these operations-based actions can often be infused with the full Mindset.

ALL KIDS ARE GOOD (HOW I VIEW ALL KIDS)

You already know how good your own kids are, but *all* kids are good. Even the kids that you wisely don't want your kids to hang out with are good. This is a belief about the innate, unchangeable nature of all children and has nothing to do with their behavior.

Remember, kids are not their behavior. Remind yourself to separate the behavior from the child. What they are doing right now may be a "knuckle-head behavior," or even a destructive behavior, but that behavior is not the child. That unchangeable good child is still inside, and we can always reset an undesirable behavior to "bring" the good child back.

That is a beautiful foundation to start with. It's a belief system that is hard-wired into my brain and it has been critical to my success in dealing with all kinds of challenging behaviors and all kinds of kids. This is really a sub-set of a larger global belief that all people are good.

We all went to school with kids who consistently exhibited distressing or undesirable behaviors. Can you think of one or two really annoying kids from your childhood?

Well, we still see them today: at our kids' school, on the soccer field, or at the daycare center. We are not going to deal with the causes of those behaviors, but it may be helpful to remember that every behavior happens for a reason. And you may not know what that reason is — even when you *think* you do.

Whatever you feel about other kids, you have the potential to broadcast to your own kids. This sounds overly simplistic, but it is an important piece of our personal hard wiring. If a dad doesn't like some kid because she was rude to a teacher, or because she was mean during a soccer game, his own child can wonder, *Is Dad going to stop loving me when I do something wrong?*

The challenge here is for you to view all kids as separate from their behavior — and to make that distinction clearly. This will help you to do the same for your own kids, which will help communicate unconditional love to them, letting them know that you will love them regardless of their behavior. They will know that you still love them even when their behavior disappoints you, and they can never "do" anything to lose that love.

Remember, kids are always observing your actions and tuning into your unspoken, unconscious beliefs. It is possible that they may not read you accurately, or they may attach the wrong meaning to something that you do. So the more they see from you that kids are innately good and loveable, the less insecure they will feel about the possibility of losing your love.

I'm not talking about your actions here: the rest of the book deals with that. This deals directly with your conscious and unconscious beliefs. Not what you think you should believe, but what you *actually* believe.

This is high-level stuff, but the more you can cultivate this distinction between behavior and child, the easier it will be to increase the balance of your child's Positive Relationship Savings Account all of the time. Developing and actively living this distinction will dramatically increase the interest rate of your PRSA, which will give you a much higher return on investment (ROI) on *all* of your positive deposits.

RESPECT (HOW I TREAT ALL KIDS)

This is the one element of the Mindset that will bankrupt your child's Positive Relationship Savings Account if you violate it. This is the where emotional scars are made.

While "all kids are good" is how I view all kids, "respect" is how I treat kids — all kids, all the time. This applies to very young children and teenagers alike. And to everyone you ever met.

As children get older, their respect-radar becomes finely tuned and highly sensitive to whether you are respecting them or not. It is built into their genetics to pay attention to their parents: Navy SEALs, remember? They are paying very close attention, and kids know when we treat them with respect — or not. And make no mistake, you either succeed or fail based upon *their* perception.

As a teacher, I had a rule in my classroom that the kids had to treat one another with respect. Sometimes a student had a hard time getting past the fact that Jeff had just beaned him with a ball on the playground. But the rule in the classroom was that they had to treat everyone with at least simulated respect, so that it looked like they were respecting the other person. They knew that I expected them to behave civilly even when they had been wronged. But simulated respect is no substitute for actual respect. You know from your own experience if someone is respecting you. Or not.

It's especially important to be mindful of respect during those times you need to be strict. Even when kids had done really bad things and I had to hand them off to the police, I was still careful not to affront their dignity. Their behavior may have been terrible, but they were not terrible themselves. I know I am preaching to the choir here, but remember how easy it is as humans to develop auto-responses that we are unaware of.

GIVING RESPECT VS. EARNING RESPECT

A few parents have hinted that Resetology™ worked so well for me because I had the "authority" of being principal. Please allow me to add some information that they were not aware of. First, the compliant respect for authority that they are referring to may be found in some schools, in some neighborhoods, but not where I worked. In those high-poverty neighborhoods, respect of any kind (especially respect for authority) is not freely given — it's earned. I worked in neighborhoods where respect was not given automatically to anyone: not to parents, not even to police officers, and certainly not to a guy in a suit with the title of principal or vice principal. I frequently had police officers shake their heads after dealing with the same child I had just dealt with and say, "I don't know how you do it." And second, parents have far more potential authority over their children than the best principal could ever command.

BE AN ACTOR, NOT A REACTOR (KEEP THE REMOTE CONTROL)

Does the battle for the TV remote control ever surface in your home? Remote controls are powerful little devices. You press a button and the TV immediately responds to your desires. Press one button and the channel changes. Press another button and the volume increases. You have total control over the TV.

As humans, we often behave similarly to the TV. Someone presses one of our "buttons" and we act. Actually, we Re-Act. Does your child ever push your buttons? Sometimes it seems like our kids have their very own daddy and mommy remote control. They push a button and dad reacts. They push another button and mom reacts.

When I react to others I give away all of my control and I cease to be the master of my own actions. When I was in high school, I read a story in one of John Powell's books (he wrote many wonderful books on connecting and being human) that I've retold more than any other story. In fact, I told this story to so many of the kids who ended up in my office that I cannot remember sharing it with any one specific child.

When I retell the story, I say it in first person (as though it were me) because I find it has more impact on kids:

was visiting a friend in New York City. We met at his office, then on our way to get coffee we stopped at a newsstand to buy a morning paper. He greeted the vendor cheerfully and was rewarded with a rude snort as the vendor turned away, ignoring him to help other customers who had come in after us. Eventually my friend got his paper when the vendor rudely shoved it in his face. My friend said, "Have a wonderful day," and we turned away. After we had gone a few steps, I asked him, "Is he always this rude to you?"

"Yes, I'm afraid he is," he said.

"But you were so nice to him and he treated you like a jerk – he was totally rude to you. How come you weren't a jerk back to him?"

I'll never forget what he said: "Because I choose to be an actor, not a reactor. I don't want someone else to control my behavior. I decide who I want to be as a person, and then I show up as that person all day – to everyone – regardless of how they treat me."

I would then process the story with them. I explained to the kids that when I live in reaction I give my remote control to everyone I meet, and allow them to control my behavior:

➥ If this person treats me nicely, then I treat them nicely.
➥ If this person treats me rudely, then I am rude to them.
➥ If she treats me like a jerk, then I treat her like a jerk.
➥ If this person is happy to see me, then I am happy to see them.
➥ This person ignores me, so I ignore them.
➥ This person smiles at me, so I smile at them.

As they listened to this perspective, many middle-schoolers began to think about how they interacted with others in their own lives. That reflection often manifested itself on their faces with a look of cognitive dissonance that said, "You mean there's a different way to act?" While middle-schoolers in general are pretty proficient reactors, they aren't the only ones. I still give my remote control away in reaction far too often.

I know that you do not wake up in the morning thinking, *I am so looking forward to getting frustrated with my kids' behavior today!* But still it happens. Don't be hard on yourself.

You work in the most challenging profession on the planet: parenting! There is no other profession so relentlessly demanding; nothing that keeps coming at you, nothing that requires more of *you*, and there is no other vocation that demands more personal sacrifice on a consistent, daily basis, 24 hours a day, seven days a week. Nothing comes even close! You have already earned my respect (seriously) because you are a parent who desires to gain more insights and tools to assist you on this challenging path. And because you're committed enough to read this far, I can tell you that your kids are very lucky little people!

As you continue to cultivate your parenting mindset, here is a suggestion for a proactive way to start your day. Begin each day by choosing and naming the emotions you want to experience. As you move through your day, don't let anyone or any circumstance tempt you to react in any other emotion. If you want this particular day to be full of peace and acceptance, set your sights on those emotions from the moment you wake up.

I frequently hear moms and dads say after attending a training session, "Wow, I've been parenting in reaction mode as a parent — it's all I do." It's so easy to fall into this; we all do to varying degrees at times in our lives. Now you can choose something different.

I want to share a quick word about power struggles. Parenting in reaction can easily lead you into a power struggle. I bring this up for two reasons:

1. To encourage you to avoid all power-struggle conversations, because as soon as you open your mouth to participate in that power struggle, you've already lost. Take the high, mature, and calm road.

2. Both you and your child may want to "exit" out of an intense power-struggle interaction, but neither of you knows how. Resetology™ provides that quick exit, that escape hatch for both of you if you need it.

DON'T TAKE IT PERSONALLY

Before we leave this Not So Fast section, let me remind you that superheroes are not always popular. You know from the movies that they are often under-appreciated and even publically scorned for their altruistic efforts to help others.

Parents are superheroes, too: the most incognito kind. Do you ever feel unpopular in your house? Of course you do — you're a parent. It can help to remember that when kids are mad, they usually aren't mad at you personally. They're mad at your behavior: at your mature, responsible parenting behavior. They're mad at what you are making them do or what you are trying to keep them from doing.

And sometimes they may say mean things.

Put up your superhero force field and become impervious to their seemingly hurtful remarks; deflect the insults and ingratitude. When you address inappropriate comments or tone of voice, don't give them your power. Don't take it personally.

I admit I am still insecure about several things in my life and maybe you are, too. It can be easy for me to allow the angry remarks of others to ignite my insecurities and to take them personally. I know how easy that is. So, remind yourself that superheroes aren't always popular. It's part of the job. Chalk it up as one of the countless sacrifices that good parents (and superheroes) have to make.

It can also be helpful to remember that kids are not their behavior. None of us is. We all have our good selves we can draw upon at any time. We are all trying to figure this life thing out. I mess up every day. Kids do, too.

As kids get older, when they get upset, remember that what you think they are upset about may not be what they are actually upset about. Give yourself permission to not know what's going on inside their heads. You don't have to have all the answers: reading minds is likely not a superpower you are gifted with.

You also don't need your kids to think you are perfect, because *that gives them the glorious permission to be imperfect, too.* Modeling for them what to do with their imperfections, how to handle the bumps in the road, may be one of the more useful and valuable things you can do for them.

Your kids are going to do things that make you proud, and they are going to do things that disappoint you and hurt your feelings. Here's how I recommend you store those memories:

Forget the negative memories like a dog
(cultivate a short memory for their wrongs and disappointments)

Remember the good memories like an elephant
(cultivate a long memory for their successes and joys)

CHAPTER 11
What You Really Long For

OK, YOUR SANDALS ARE OFF – EITHER METAPHORICALLY OR LITERALLY – AND YOU are ready to engage the smaller or younger human being in front of you. Once your sandals are off and you are present, you may choose to go no further. That can be more than enough and may be your entire outcome for an interaction. Your humble presence will engage them at an unconscious level. But sometimes, you will want to connect further. In this section we're going to focus on crossing the gap to engage your child.

In order to engage them further you have to cross the gap between two separate individual people: between you and your child. I am going to show you two proven paths to engagement using Smile Resetters and **conversations.** Yes, conversations. For decades I've witnessed parents trying to engage their children with impotent attempts at conversation. I'm going to give you some simple new ways to spark deeper dialogue.

Sometimes your desired outcome may simply be to share a fun interaction with your child, which is a very noble outcome. You aren't looking to discover any information about their life, and you are not trying to communicate anything specific to them. You just want to have fun *with* them. That's where Smile Resetters come in.

The third stage in developing the Resetology™ Mindset is engaging to connect with your child. There are three elements:

- ➡ Having fun with vs making fun of
- ➡ Connecting with a real conversation
- ➡ Finding the fun

HAVING FUN WITH *VS* MAKING FUN OF

IMPORTANT: There's a fine line between having fun *with* and making fun *of.*

Before you engage you need to know that there's a critical difference between having fun *with* and making fun *of.* One adds to the Positive Relationship Savings Account and builds the child up. The other bankrupts the PRSA and leaves emotional scars. One is positive, the other is tragic. You've always got to be aware not to stray over that line, but there's an easy way to tell the difference.

Emotional scars can be large or small and can occur over time or in a thoughtless instant. And they can happen without your knowledge. When we see a parent screaming at a child in public, we can easily recognize the potential for emotional scarring in that moment. Scarring is a relative term: even small remarks or incidents can be hurtful and leave a "mark."

Take a moment to think back to an emotional scar from your own life that was caused by words said to you by an adult, maybe your parents. Did the person who said the hurtful words know that they were hurting your feelings, or were they completely unaware of what they had just done to you? It may have happened when they thought they were just teasing and having fun. Little did they know that the hurt you felt from those words could be lingering and impactful.

If you have any doubts about whether something might not be fun for both of you, it's better to pass. Have fun, but avoid leaving scars at all costs. Practice emotional scar prevention: it is better to miss an opportunity to be funny (which makes you feel good) than to accidentally offend or hurt your child.

Note: These techniques can be used to at least improve most relationships and situations. I'm not talking about criminal or grossly negligent behaviors. Resetology™ is not a substitute for professional counseling when it is necessary.

Having fun *with* means that you are entering into the fun situation with the child as an equal partner in the fun-ness, an equal collaborator, a co-creator in the humor of this fun moment.

There's an easy way to tell if you are having fun *with*: **you are both laughing and both smiling real smiles**. Of course, a child can always paint a fake smile on their face, so you have to be aware. Be especially alert if they are not smiling when you think they should be smiling.

Always be aware when laughing at your children, even when a situation is downright funny. If your laughter hurts their feelings, you've just made a withdrawal from their Positive Relationship Savings Account . If you are in any way selfish in your intentions while having fun — if you say or think, "Ha! Look what she did!" Or, "Look what I did to him!" — that's dangerous ground, and that can be something that a child remembers for life.

If you think doing something might be funny, for the sake of your child, think ahead to the conclusion *before* you do it. Picture in your mind whether what you are considering doing will leave you both smiling — on the outside *and* on the inside. Think about this ahead of time so you don't accidentally paint yourself into a situation that makes them feel bad.

The greater the level of connection and rapport that you enjoy with your child (from *their* perspective, not from yours) the greater the latitude you have to venture carefully into the teasing realm. But only go there carefully and intentionally, never accidentally. Teasing can be fun, but it is super easy for it to go over the line without you knowing that it ceased to be fun for your child. Again, think of the times in your own life when teasing was fun and those times when it may have been hurtful. Tread with caution!

I want you to use this information to strengthen your own awareness that having fun can cross the line and become hurtful. Once you are reminded of this, however, **I want you to focus on having fun**! One of my main intentions for Resetology™ is for you to have even more fun with your kids than you ever thought possible. Just be aware.

Since you are human, you are going to mess up. When you mess up there are two Mindset habits (Forgive and PhD Apology) coming up in Chapter 12 that will serve you tremendously.

A Note About Negative Humor

My friends and I used to use a lot of negative humor with each other, but I've tried to eliminate it. Even though I know my friends really well, it is impossible for me to know exactly how a put-down from me makes them feel. If you jokingly put your friends down, be very careful to exclude that negative joking style from the humor you share with your kids. In fact, you will probably lose nothing by eliminating negative humor from your life completely.

CONNECT WITH A REAL CONVERSATION

Can you remember going on a date with someone you really liked and found yourself asking more interesting questions and telling your own stories with a bit more flair and enthusiasm? Don't your kids deserve that same level of engagement and presence?

Would you like to know more about your child: what concerns them, how the relationships with their friends are going, what they are they are looking forward to? Have your sincere attempts at engaging your child in conversation ever been rewarded with disappointing responses? Maybe this conversation sounds familiar:

> How was school today?
> *Fine.*
> What did you learn today?
> *Nothing.*
> Who did you hang out with?
> *No one.*

Fine. Nothing. No one.

The problem is that, all too often, these actually are the precise answers to your questions. You see, in the mind of your child, these are tired questions. Although these questions are sincere attempts to connect with your kids, this is a tired conversation … a lazy conversation … a conversation on auto-pilot.

What's your real reason for asking how their day went, anyway? While you may be genuinely interested in the details of their day, the primary goal of the conversation is to have a shared moment of connection. Sometimes you might catch your kids in a chatty mood when the tired old questions actually work. But if it doesn't work, why keep doing it? Why not guide them to a better mood or entice them with a more interesting conversation?

There are two ways to approach this.

1. Beginning Level: Ask Better Questions

This is gold, right here. Ask creative questions and you'll get different responses. You can always find a different doorway to enter a conversation. For example …

The Best Fun Question of All Time. Here's a great question that I've used with kids of all ages who are old enough to be familiar with some superheroes.

I was driving a truck full of high-school kids to the Colorado River for a week of youth group leadership training. As we were driving through the desert, the conversation lagged and I wouldn't let them listen to iPods if they rode with me. So I pulled out the "Best Fun Question of All Time"!

"All right," I said, "everyone has to answer this question. If you could have any superhero power, what would it be? And why?" They couldn't reveal their power until they had thought of the answers to both questions.

After they had all shared, one of the kids asked, "Okay, JimHouse [all of the teens pronounced my first and last name together as one word], which superhero power would you pick?" I was silent for minute and then I took my favorite food in the world and turned it into a superhero power.

"My power would be the ability to spontaneously create a milkshake at any time — any flavor."

They laughed and one of the teens asked, "What good are milkshake powers?"

I said, "What problem or situation in the world would not be made better by the introduction of milkshakes?"

On the spot I invented "Milkshake Man"; I even created special sound effects for him. For the rest of the week, and even to this day, Milkshakes and Milkshake Man are a part of our banter.

This is a great question/activity to do with more than one child, but one kid is fine. Think about your answer in advance. Maybe you could even pick two superhero powers, or invent your own original superhero power before you ask them. And have fun!

I strongly encourage you to become aware of the questions you ask your kids to see if you are trying to start any tired conversations. And then ask new and creative questions.

There is even a better way to break through tired conversations to connect.

2. Advanced Level: Share Yourself

"How was your day?" can sound overwhelming to older kids because during the day they had 3000 thoughts, 37 different conversations, and a variety of classroom learning experiences — many of which may have seemed boring or torturous. So they can easily suffer from a version of "blank-page syndrome", where your seemingly benign question has far too many possible answers to sort through. They may be thinking, "Where do I even start to decide what to share with my parents?" It's much easier for them to just shut down the question with a one-word answer.

Consider sharing a piece of your own story, unsolicited, so they have a story to react to.

This works with kids of most any age, as long as the story you share connects with their age. By telling a story, you pull them in; kids are actually very curious about your life, but they don't think or know how to ask. Don't worry if they roll their eyes — any time you share an authentic piece of yourself, it's an investment, and is never time wasted. Try to share something interesting, so they want to listen. Make it short. Think it up beforehand. Be vulnerable (but always appropriate).

If sharing your own personal stories is new for you, here are some thoughts to help you.

Consider saying it out loud at least once so you can edit out the boring parts, and avoid accidentally going down a path that you hadn't remembered — that's really the only thing you have to be wary of. Let me make this easy for you:

> ➡ there are no such things as typos when speaking about yourself
> ➡ you will screw up some sentences (*everyone* does); they won't notice
> ➡ you may tell the story out of order; it does not matter
> ➡ you may forget someone's name; it does not matter
> ➡ you may think you are telling it wrong; it does not matter (they've never heard the story before, so they won't know!)
> ➡ there doesn't have to be a point to the story — just share

A reminder: Sharing must always be appropriate and age appropriate.

To start off your self-disclosure stories, call up your memories of elementary, middle, and high school.

> ➡ think back to when you were the same age as your child
> ➡ talk about one of the teachers you remember
> ➡ who was your favorite teacher and why?
> ➡ what did they look like?
> ➡ did they ever compliment you?

Here's a great source of memories: school lunches!

> ➡ did you have the same thing for lunch every day?

➡ did you trade?
➡ how much did milk cost?
➡ what was your favorite hot school lunch?
➡ what was the grossest?

I used to have really thin-sliced lunchmeat, usually pastrami or turkey, on buttered wheat bread with a piece of lettuce that was often wilted by lunchtime. I liked it, but I never could get anyone to trade their Hostess Ding Dong for it.

There's treasure in the detail of your school memories:

➡ what was the name of your school?
➡ what did you like playing at recess?
➡ what was your favorite PE activity?
➡ who did you play with at recess and lunch?
➡ do you remember a story or a poem you wrote?
➡ what was your favorite picture book? Chapter book? Novel?
➡ what was hard for you at school? (Dig deep — there must have been at least one thing that was difficult or awkward)

Kids love to hear (appropriate) things you've never told anyone before: "I ate a bug once because Jeff bet me a nickel."

What if you planned and shared one new thing about yourself each day for a month? What impact do you think that would have on your children? Make a list of interesting childhood memories to share with your kids.

➡ **ENGAGE:**
For more conversation starting prompts and ideas, visit
http://www.resetology.com/book/downloads

Guide To Self-Disclosure

When you initiate conversation by sharing some of your own story, your kids will listen and interpret through their own story (it's how we all interpret the stories, songs, and movies we encounter). This may remind them of something from their day, or may prompt them to ask clarifying questions. And how cool is that, when you have your own kids asking you about your life?

The stories don't have to be about your distant past; they just need to have some element of interest, or emotion, or failure. But don't be preachy. Not even a bit! Kids can sniff that from 1,000 miles away. If you have a moral to your story, let them deduce it on their own.

If your story is greeted by silence, I encourage you to hold the silence. Hold it for a long time. Ten seconds will seem like an eternity, especially if you've you just shared something vulnerable. But remember: your sharing is a pure gift to your children, and you give them your story with no expectation that they will reward you with a "Wow!" or "I never knew that about you," or any feedback whatsoever.

The ultimate hope is that they are encouraged to share something of themselves with you. It could be as benign as "Brenda Chatsworth threw up in class today," or something deeper like, "I'm afraid I won't ever have a boyfriend." Try very hard to just receive whatever they say without trying to quantify how big a sharing you've inspired, as though you were measuring the size of a fish you just caught. Even though you may be sharing in the hope of starting a conversation, the intention of sharing yourself is always to gift them.

Don't expect them to become captivated by your story; depending on their age, they will process the information very differently. But regardless of their age, they will all subconsciously accept it as pure gift, so long as it's true (even though you don't always have to give all the details), and you lead with the intention of giving them a piece of you, and you are not specifically trying to manipulate them into talking.

If they say nothing or joke about what you said, you can always say:

➡ "I just wanted to share that with you." (or)
➡ "I just wanted to share that with you, because I love you." (or)
➡ "I just wanted to share that with you, because I want you to know this about me."

Or just say nothing.

And be okay with that. Remember, you offer a gift with no expectation of getting anything for yourself. There is no downside to sharing your stories and yourself when done appropriately.

Pay attention when they talk – and remember what they say

Congratulations: you asked better questions or you gifted your child with a story from your past and that caused them to share some information with you. That's amazing. Now comes an equally important part: *listen.*

And then listen some more.

Try to remember what they tell you. If you learn something new, write it down as soon as you can so you can make a casual and appropriate reference to it later on. Your Positive Relationship Savings Account will rise again when your kids realize you were paying attention. Again, be appropriate: some things should not be shared at all or with certain people around.

FIND THE FUN

"I'd forgotten how to have fun as a parent," gushed an excited dad after a coaching session.

The best family memories are born in moments of fun. If you are willing to risk embarrassment (being perceived as silly) you will open a world of opportunities for positive and humorous interactions with your children.

Get over yourself! Give your kids the gift of embarrassing yourself in front of them. You do your kids a disservice by trying to be perfect in front of them all of the time. It gives them a grossly unrealistic expectation to try to live up to.

What gets me out of bed in the morning is helping families to have more fun together.

Finding fun is the gold standard for investing. There are few actions you can take that will fill up your Positive Relationship Savings Account faster and higher than shared experiences of fun. Cultivate smiles in your family. Make this a mission!

You've heard it said that there's a silver lining in every circumstance. While I tend to be a silver-lining guy, I also believe there's a **"fun lining"** in most every circumstance. I always look for the fun lining; there is fun to be had everywhere. And you don't usually have to look very far. It lies latent, just waiting to be awakened in every moment. And it's almost always appropriate to do so.

Laughter is the great equalizer. It dissolves age and role differences and provides wide access to a shared experience. Humor is also a powerful emotional solvent: it can quickly dissolve intense emotional grime. Humor is a great way to manifest both the dramatic and the unexpected. If you can get someone to laugh — game over!

How To Find the Fun

Create and activate a special radar for fun moments. Be on the lookout for them, focus on them, invent them whenever you see an opening. Make a funny face at your child that no one else can see: a private, shared fun moment. When you notice a fun moment, stop and submerse yourself in it with your kids.

When something funny happens, whenever you have a shared funny moment, keep track of it. Write it down in your Family Fun Archive: a Word doc, a database, a notebook or scrapbook that you keep with other family treasures, like your photo albums.

Jokes

Many of my good friends are superb joke tellers; they're able to silence a room once they start telling a joke because everyone wants to hear it. Me, on the other hand … I sometimes screw up punch lines. In fact, one of my gifted joke-telling friends once said of me (in an attempt to rescue me from the awkward silence I forced upon the group with a crappy retelling of a joke) that I had perfected the telling of the "pseudo-joke": it has the same structure, major and minor premise, and punch line as a joke — it's just not funny.

There are all kinds of jokes, but my favorite ones without a doubt are corny ones. I love telling the corny jokes that my Dad used to tell. Many of them are "groaners", but they work great in many situations because my intention is clearly not to declare, "Hey, look how funny I am!" I think that people like me who are not naturally funny actually have a leg up on the really funny guys, because it doesn't matter if the kid laughs or not. Confident and corny with a mischievous twinkle in my eye is a powerful resetting posture. This is one of my favorites: feel free to use it!

Q. What do you call a deer with no eyes?

A. No idear. (No-eye deer!)

Okay, I can hear your groans, but you did smile a little bit, didn't you?

You don't have to go corny, especially if you are actually capable of telling jokes well. There are lots of resources for age-appropriate jokes, but one of my favorites is the Prairie Home Companion's annual joke show. You can find a link to it at www.Resetology.com/book/downloads

We all have particular tastes in the type of humor that tickles our funny bone. Do you know what makes your child laugh? That's really useful information!

I want to provide you with a few guardrails before you unleash your fun-ness on your family and the world.

1. Humor must always be appropriate
Take the high road, always.

2. Important note about teasing
I know we already talked about it, so this is just a gentle reminder. The more full your Positive Relationship Savings Account is, the greater the level of rapport that you enjoy with your child (from their perspective, not from yours), and the greater the latitude you have to venture carefully into the teasing realm. But only go there carefully and intentionally, never accidentally. Teasing can be fun, but it is super easy for it to go over the line without knowing that it has ceased to be fun for the child. You can both have some fun with gentle teasing – just tread with caution!

3. Never make fun of one person to make another person laugh
(Even when it's just family and friends around.) We can't see inside someone else's head to determine how they are receiving our message and what meaning they are attaching to it. Communication is always complex and there are no guarantees that your child will receive the message in the same way that you intended it. If there is even a remote chance that one child will not enjoy it, don't do it. Was there ever a time when someone made fun of you – and they may not have even known it?

4. There's a fine line between making fun of and having fun with
Again, one is a shared experience, and the other is selfish and tragic. Am I trying to bring the attention to me? It's better to skip it than to risk a hurtful moment that will leave a mark. Don't get carried away and lose sight of this.

When you reach the end of this book, you'll see that the very last story is about how a troubled young man's life was forever changed because I told him a joke. Do not underestimate the power of humor!

Sing

I try not to use the word "should" very much, but I'm going to make an exception and say that you should sing. Sing more. Sing often — to yourself and to your kids. Singing is good for the soul. Some of the best memories of my life involve singing.

I grew up listening to and singing along with great albums and (yes, tapes!). We wore out lots of albums on the record player! My dad sang in a barbershop quartet, so we always heard him practicing the bass part for his latest repertoire.

Each summer when we were young, we drove from San Diego to Montana, all five of us crammed into a small Datsun sedan. To pass the time, Dad would teach us a new song. We would sing it together until we knew the words and the melody, and then we would try to sing it as a round. Sometimes it was pretty good, sometimes it was a train wreck, but it was always fun!

One of my favorite memories of my dad was watching him lead group singing at huge campfires in Indian Guides, Boy Scout camp, or camping with friends. My brother Will and I eventually started singing in barbershop quartets too, and I can tell you that few activities from my life have provided me with as much fun.

My singing didn't stop when I went to work. I used to sing all the time when I worked at schools. As a teacher I used singing as an integral and powerful part of my classroom management system. As a principal I sang to calm kids and keep the busy office environment playful. There are several ways you can use singing to create more fun in your family.

Sing just for fun
I think singing by yourself just for fun is a lost art. It doesn't matter if you think you have a great voice, or if you think your voice is less than stellar. Chances are pretty good that you already sing along when your favorite song comes on the radio in the car. So consider this your invitation to bust it out more often. Singing just for fun is a whole lot of, well … fun!

Sing with your child
Singing a song together with another person (or 150 other people) envelopes both of you inside a shared experience of fun. Seriously, I think there's potential for a doctoral-level study here.

Song selection
Obviously, age will be a factor here. The younger your kids are, the easier it will be to find songs. Choose songs that they like to sing. And don't be afraid to sing some of your favorite songs, including your "oldies". Folk songs and holiday songs are generally pretty easy to sing. Country songs tend to have simple, sing-able melodies. You can even make up songs: I do it all the time.

I know very little about rap music but I like rap that involves melody. I have great respect for rappers' talent, and I'm probably going to incur the wrath of the rap world by saying this, but I'm not encouraging you to sing rap songs that have no melody. I believe there is magic in a good melody. It's why melodies get stuck in our brains. Rhythm can be catchy, too: I just believe it's a different type of shared experience. Perhaps it's because you can harmonize with a melody, but not with talking. Even if you don't add harmony, a naked melody alone is always rich with the latent possibility of simple or complex harmonies. And you don't have to speak a certain language in order to connect with or be moved by a melody.

I recommend that you share your own favorite music with your kids, especially the music you liked when you were their age. And for the love of Mike, please make sure that at least some of that music has a melody. I think you are missing out on a *great* opportunity if your kids are not "burdened" by your oldies every now and then. Fill your house with song!

Singing can also be a very powerful Resetter. In Chapter 5, you read how I used an old crooner's song to tame a savage crowd.

Movies

Kids often memorize favorite lines from funny movies; for me it was the famous lines from the movie *Monty Python and the Holy Grail.* I had heard and memorized most of the funny lines from the soundtrack years before I ever saw the movie.

Pay attention to your child's favorite movies. Find the funny lines from the movies you watch together. Look for times to toss out these already funny lines!

SMILE RESETTERS

There's a whole category of fun Smile Resetters, which have no objective other than creating a shared experience of fun. Read more about these in Chapter 12.

LEMONS TO LEMONADE?

Sometimes the best time to create fun is when it seems farthest away. I'm not talking about cracking knock-knock jokes at a funeral. But in those situations where the lemons prevail and when pouty faces abound, it often doesn't take a whole lot of effort to reset the situation. When life gives you lemons, make lemonade — or lemon meringue milkshakes!

You can do this, too!

Here are a few stories from parents like you, and one child, who "found the fun" in difficult situations and made lemonade out of lemons.

Jessica's Story

Homework gets such a bad rap that, even before she was assigned any, my eldest daughter had convinced herself that she hated it. It didn't matter that the work she eventually brought home was rather easy worksheets that closely resembled the summer work that I (mean mommy that I am) had made her do during the months that preceded her entry into second grade.

Every afternoon of her second-grade school year, I was treated to groans and moans when I asked what homework she had to get done. Every afternoon of her second-grade school year ended with her sitting on the floor of her playroom closet as she sobbed quietly over her math homework. All of my offers of help were rebuffed emphatically. Any of my offers of corrections when I checked her work were greeted with screams of frustration.

To say that I wasn't looking forward to third-grade homework would be an understatement.

The year started off with a nice easy homework-free week and just a gentle request from the teacher to have the kids read and practice math facts every afternoon. That was easy. It was an echo of what I'd had both kids do all summer. Books were read in cozy nooks and math facts were practiced unwittingly as they played math games on the iPad. Smiles all around.

And then the "real" homework started coming home. And I started to hold my breath.

Before the histrionics had even a chance to get started I said, as off-handedly as I could, "Hey, when you're done with the homework you have to get done, we can all play a game together."

Now, it has to be said that I'm not one to sit and play games with the kids. That's my husband's job. I provide and care for everyone; he plays. It's a perfect trade. But I had a hunch that it would be just enough of an incentive to get her motivated. "I'm even happy to help so it goes faster!" I added.

Old habits die hard; so she grabbed her math book and went off to hide, but it wasn't long before she tiptoed into my office and quietly asked for help. I stopped what I was doing and gave her my undivided attention (nothing like a little positive reinforcement) and in no time at all the page of math was done.

"Now we can go play a game?" she asked, hesitating a bit, not entirely convinced that I would still be willing to play.

"Yup! Go find a deck of cards; I want to teach you a new game."

The year before, getting through homework would have reduced her to tears, me to tearing out my hair, and my younger daughter to begging for some attention herself. That day, my husband walked in to find us sitting around the dining room table playing a convoluted version of the classic card game War.

"Daddy! Daddy! We're playing War! Everyone puts down two cards and we add them up! The person with the highest number wins all the cards!"

I didn't tell them that they were really still doing homework and practicing their math facts. I let them just think they were playing a game. We haven't had a homework tantrum since and everyone's math skills are improving. Win–win all around really.

– Jessica Rosenberg (http://www.itsjessicaslife.com)

Pam's Story

Anyone with children clearly knows that they are in our lives to teach us, not the other way around.

Our youngest played football for the first time at the age of five. It was so much more intense than we ever could have imagined. In addition to the 7:30am arrival time for Saturday morning games that were often 45 min away, our little Ben was consistently out there blocking kids twice his size.

The great thing about Ben, though, is that he isn't fazed by things like that. It doesn't matter to him that the kids are bigger than him and often push him down. His job is to get the flag belonging to the guy with the ball and, God bless him, he's not about to let anyone stand in the way.

One of his best plays of the season happened when he got the other team's flag at fourth and goal, forcing them to punt–or whatever five-year-olds to do when they turn the ball over on downs. You would have thought he had just won the Super Bowl. He started high-fiving everyone in his sight, and when he ran out of people on the field, he came off to the sidelines and starting high-fiving everyone there.

While there was a great play here and there, Ben's team often struggled in their league. His team was new to our area, which meant the kids on Ben's team were younger, smaller and newer to the game than most of the other teams they played. This almost inevitably translated to a blow-out victory by the other team.

At the end of each game, my husband and I would cringe at the moment when Ben looked up at us enthusiastically and ask, "Did we win?" After about two weeks of dodging the question, we finally starting answering him, reminding him that what was important was to have fun and to try his best (and of course, my main concern, to stay safe).

Amazingly, regardless of what we told Ben about the final score, he would walk around the rest of the day telling anyone in his path that he won his football game that day. At first, we would correct him, reminding him gently that it wasn't about winning or losing but, rather, about having fun and working hard.

After several weeks of Ben announcing that his team won games that they didn't, we started to get concerned.

However, we had another thought: what if Ben was onto something? Does it really matter what the score was, in reality, if our son is happy and wants to think he really did win? What's more important in the long run: pushing reality in his face or fostering his positive psychology and confidence?

After all, how often do we, as adults, beat ourselves up and tell ourselves we lost, when in fact we really did win? Or focus on what we didn't do perfectly, rather than what we did right?

By Ben's perception, he really did win. He tried hard, he had fun, he stayed safe and he was a good sport. Isn't that what we had been trying to teach him all season? So who were we to say that he has to say he won or lost by our rules or perception?

Now that the season has ended, we realize that maybe we're the ones who discovered the most meaningful lessons from Ben's first season of football. In the words of Jackson Browne, "Forget About the Losses, You Exaggerate the Wins!"

—*Pam Hendrickson*, pamhendrickson.com

Nikki's Story

The holidays are a time for family and traditions and it's difficult that we live away from some of our extended family. We normally travel to Arizona for Thanksgiving and Christmas but last year we were unable to go. Instead we decided to host a small dinner at our home and spent the week planning for the event.

Thanksgiving morning dawned and my three kids were in rare form. They fought with one another over everything – what to watch on TV, who ate the last of the cereal, who was sitting in *their* spot on the couch. When they weren't arguing with one another, they complained to me about being bored and wanted to know what time dinner would be served.

"Not for nine hours," I said in my best sing-song voice.

Nine hours.

It was going to be a very long day.

My first instinct was to send them to clean their rooms. That would certainly keep them busy and out of earshot. But I wanted to keep the focus on Thanksgiving and really concentrate on what the holiday means. I pulled out a large piece of heavy white poster board and gathered some markers to put on the dining room table. In the middle of the board I wrote in large block letters:

I AM THANKFUL FOR . . .

I then called the kids over and told them to decorate the rest. They paused, gave me a strange look, and then the urge to get crafting took hold and the fun began.

They drew pictures, they wrote words, and they colored in letters. They wrote that they were thankful for Mom and Dad, for each other, for their teachers. One child was thankful for friends, another for her computer, and another for her books. They worked together to think of ideas and had fun brainstorming their favorite foods and toys.

At the end they were proud to show off their handiwork. It was beautiful. I kept it out all day for them to show off when guests arrived. I even put it on a shelf and kept it visible for several months as a reminder to them to appreciate all the things they do have.

It's a tradition that started on a whim and it's a tradition I would like to implement every year on Thanksgiving. I imagine some things will be different this year – and some things will remain the same. But it will always be fun.

–*Nikki Katz*, nikkikatz.com

➡️ **ENGAGE:** Share your stories with us

Do you have your own "Lemons to Lemonade" story that you would like to share with us? There are a couple of reasons to share your stories:

Once again, your story may reveal to another parent a new way for them to handle a similar situation. Reflecting on your own story will strengthen your own ability to continue to see the potential lemonade in future "lemony" situations you encounter.

We may even share your story in the blog, on the website, or in a future book (with your permission, of course).

Every story submitted will receive a personal thank you message from me.

Submit stores/videos at http://www.resetology.com/share-your-story

CHAPTER 12

Repair and Restore

THE FOURTH AND FINAL STAGE IN DEVELOPING THE RESETOLOGY™ MINDSET is repairing and restoring to connect with your child. There are five elements:

- → Everyday Apology
- → PhD Apology
- → Suspend Judgment
- → Smile Resetters
- → Forgive

It eventually happens to all of us at some point in all of our relationships — we screw up in some way. But that does not spell the end of the relationship. In fact, when you take the authentic steps toward repairing and restoring, it's even possible that you may have a stronger connection on the other side. Let's begin with Repairing.

APOLOGIZE

They screw up: forgive
You screw up: apologize – and ask forgiveness

Apologizing is the sacred and necessary first step in repairing and restoring a damaged relationship. Apologies are gold. There is profound healing power in the words "I'm sorry." I can't tell you how many serious and small problems arise between kids every day on the playground at both elementary and middle schools. What I can tell you is how many of those problems vaporized and vanished just because I was able to get one student to apologize to another. Situation closed. No angry residue. No resentment. Magical.

While the short-term goal of apologizing is concerned with repairing and restoring a broken relationship, the long-term value of apologizing to your kids is immense. By apologizing to your kids, you model for them how to apologize themselves. This is another huge legacy you will gift your kids with, and it will serve them tremendously in developing rich relationships for the rest of their lives.

I believe that the school playground is a microcosm of human interaction. Sometimes the dynamics in our families can resemble the dynamics in a playground at recess. We ignore one another, we hurt one anothers' feelings, we offend one another, we get mad at one another, and we disappoint one another.

Here's the deal: you are going to screw up; it's unavoidable. So when you do, be strong enough to apologize. You get angry and then regret it, so apologize. You raise your voice and regret it, so apologize. You say something hurtful and regret it, so apologize. You forget something important and regret it — apologize.

Make the most out of every apology, even for small infractions, because you are training your children to be good apologizers themselves. Be sincere — don't fake it. (Remember: Navy SEALs.)

Everyday Apology

Physiology
- ⇒ face your child
- ⇒ be present
- ⇒ get eye contact
- ⇒ once you get eye contact and before you apologize, pause briefly and silently say, "I love you," with your eyes (think the words in your head)

Focus
- ➡ try to feel what they are feeling: have empathy
- ➡ say: "I'm sorry I ..."
- ➡ take responsibility for what you did: admit it, fess up
- ➡ name the consequences of your actions and acknowledge how it hurt them
- ➡ ask for forgiveness; this returns power to the hurt child
- ➡ don't get defensive
- ➡ let it be over and done with

Make sure that you graciously accept any apologies that your child makes to you. Say thank you and let it be the end. More teaching can come later if necessary.

PhD Apology: When You Really Screw Up

Many parents have admitted to me that they sometimes have very negative feelings toward their kids. I suspect that most parents deal with this to some degree at times. When your frustration with your child's misbehavior crosses over to ill feelings toward your child, even briefly, it's easy to screw up and say something you regret.

Some screw-ups are bigger than others. Some screw-ups create gaping rifts in our relationships and may even leave emotional scars (or scratches) that will require some intentional repairing. For those really big screw-ups, you need to be intentional about planning your apology. It's okay to apologize as soon as you recognize the need, then go away and spend the time necessary to plan an intentional apology to share with them later. This will take some time. You have to put some distance between you and the situation and spend time in reflection so that you become aware of what needs to be shared.

Try to circle back to talk with your child within a day, but not before you have gone deep into both reflection and preparation.

Julie's Story

As a parent, I'm the first to admit that I'm not perfect. And parenting teenagers has been a whole new world for me. My oldest son, Sam, is generally an easy-to-get-along-with, happy kid, but this year we've been butting heads over his need for freedom and my insistence that he comply with the rules. It's totally natural and normal yet no matter how much I hear (or tell myself) that, it's still been an extremely emotional and challenging time for me as a mother.

A few months ago, in a moment of pure frustration, I told a friend of mine who doesn't have kids that I envied her decision to remain child-free. I said it during a phone conversation that I knew Sam could overhear right after a particularly frustrating argument with him. While I didn't say it in the moment with the intent to hurt him, I know on some level that was part of why I said it loud enough for him to hear it. Of course I wasn't serious and I in no way regret having my boys, but in that moment it just felt good to vent. Unfortunately, he took it very personally.

A few hours later, after he'd gone to school, I got a text message from him saying how much it had hurt his feelings and that, based on what I'd said, he felt he didn't really want to be around me for a while, preferring to stay at his dad's in the short term.

I felt horrible and called my friend Jim House (who also happens to be an expert on dealing with kids and conflict). I relayed the situation and asked his advice. Jim told me he'd recommend that I sit down and draft an apology that was absolutely exceptional to offer to my son.

He praised my skills as a powerful motivational speaker, coach, and business-woman. He then encouraged me sit down and create an apology that was completely out of this world using the same level of deep, intentional planning I would use when preparing for a big keynote speech. He challenged me to go deep and share something from my life that would communicate to my son how much he meant to me. Jim then rushed me off the phone and told me to get to work.

That afternoon after I picked Sam up from school, I was nervous and a little emotional. I told him I needed to talk to him and sat him down on the couch, next to me. I had a plan for what I wanted to say in what order but pretty much spoke from my heart about him and how I felt about being his mom.

I shared with him something I'd never told him before. I told him about the year and a half it took me to get pregnant with him and how I had started to fear I'd never be able to have a baby. It was one of the hardest things I've ever gone through.

We had been trying for so long and it felt like everyone else was pregnant. I remember Roseanne Barr was expecting and so was Princess Di and I just thought, "Everyone in the world is having a baby except me." There was one particular night when David (his dad) was on the road (he was a truck driver and gone a few nights a week) when it got overwhelming and I started to pray about it. Only this time, instead of praying to have a baby, I just surrendered and said, "You know what, God? Maybe it's not in your plan for me to be a mom. Maybe I'm supposed to do something else. Maybe I'm supposed to adopt a baby. Maybe there's something out there that I can't even imagine right now that I'm supposed to do. Whatever it is, I'm just praying for the wisdom to understand what your plan is and the strength to be able to accept it."

And then I told Sam exactly how I reacted when I found out I was pregnant.

I was home alone. My husband and my mom were on a weekend horseback riding trip. I did the test like I had so many times before and I walked out of the bathroom and set the timer. When the timer went off I remember hesitating because I didn't want to look; I was afraid I'd be disappointed again. When I finally got up the courage to look and saw that the result was positive, I literally screamed out loud. We had two terriers and they came running into the bathroom, afraid I was hurt or something. I just stood there grinning and completely amazed. And I couldn't even tell anyone because my husband and mom were gone. I had to wait two whole days before I could share the news with a single soul. It was honestly the happiest, longest two days, waiting to tell my husband that something we had both wanted for so long had finally happened.

I told Sam there had never been a mom who had been happier to hold her newborn son as I had been on the day he was born. I told him that I hadn't changed the way I felt about him, even on those days when it seemed like I didn't like him much. I said I was really sorry about what I'd said and was honest with him about why I'd said it. I told him I couldn't imagine my life without him and how much I loved him. He was blown away and it was one of the best conversations we'd had in a really long time.

I know I would have apologized even if I hadn't consulted Jim. What I also know is that I would not have shared a personal story, and I wouldn't have taken the time to reflect deeply and to prepare intentionally in the way I did to really make the conversation meaningful, and it wouldn't have had the impact it did on our relationship without Jim's advice.

–Julie Anne Jones, JulieAnneJones.com

My thanks to Julie and Sam for sharing their story. When Julie called me that day she was flustered and incredibly remorseful, and she knew she needed to do something special to begin to repair and restore the relationship with her son. I truly admire her willingness to seek out additional parenting tools and information when she needed them. Here's the framework that will allow you to create the same intentional apologies for those times when a heartfelt apology may not be enough. I call it the PhD Apology.

PhD APOLOGY

To do a high-level, PhD Apology, this is all you have to remember:

PhD = Plan + humble + Disclosure

1. **Plan.** In order for this apology to rise to the level of impact you need, you need to remove yourself from the situation, get really quiet, and spend some time planning what you are going to say – specifically what you are going to share. In this step you also plan how and when you are going to apologize. I recommend leading with the humble apology before you share your story: it will help to lower your child's guard so that they are more receptive to hearing your disclosure.

2. **humble.** (The letter "h" is intentionally not capitalized to represent the humility of dying to yourself and subduing your ego during this process.) As we talked about in Connection, remember to "remove your sandals" in humility. This is important during the planning, and especially critical while apologizing and disclosing.

3. **Disclosure.** Disclosure implies that you are revealing something new that was heretofore unknown to your child. Sharing some personal story strengthens the sincerity and impact of the apology and immediately begins to build the bridge of restoration.

    Get vulnerable. I encourage you to take out pen and paper and capture the feelings coursing through you, and then brainstorm stories about yourself that might be vulnerable and new to share with your child. Remember, this step is called "disclosure," not "share an old familiar story." You are giving them a gift, so make it truly special and meaningful.

Get present and trust your heart. Of course, you can adapt the depth and content of your sharing to be age appropriate. And don't forget to actually say, "I'm sorry." There is a deeper look at how to plan and deliver a Phd Apology below, but first let's take a closer look at the PhD Apology elements in Julie's story.

Plan. I advised Julie to invest some serious time and effort into planning her apology. When I asked Julie what her planning process had looked like, this is what she said:

> I sat in my office and looked out the window at my yard. It always helps me think. Then I thought about how much I loved Sam and how, after he was born, I had kept a journal about how much I loved him because someone had told me I would need to look back on that some day when he was a teenager. Then I got his baby book out and looked through it. It totally changed my perspective. I wrote down some notes about what I wanted to say.

Julie took time to reflect and was very purposeful about planning her apology. She even triggered memories of her son by opening his baby book and looking back at her journals. Physical props are helpful, but not necessary to accomplish this; you can simply lead yourself on a guided tour of good memories. There's a warm and loving Resetting of your heart that takes place while strolling through fond memories of your child (or anyone).

Julie approached this planning with the same level of commitment and professionalism as when she prepares to speak on a big stage to a large audience. Because she invested the time, she was able to share an incredible story directly related to healing the wound she had caused. Julie got present, dug deep, and then remembered the amazing story of her son's birth.

humble. Julie's first step in humility was her immediate recognition that she had messed up and hurt her son's feelings, and she had to fix it. Next, she humbly reached out to me, shared what had happened, and asked for guidance. She then invested her time and self in presence to reflect and discover a significant and vulnerable story to disclose to her son. Finally, she "took off her sandals" when she spoke with her son to apologize and disclose her meaningful story.

Disclosure. Julie shared herself by disclosing a heartfelt and meaningful story. She tried to come up with something that would specifically address the hurt she had caused. However, specific relevance is not necessary. What is important is that you share a new, vulnerable, significant piece of yourself. Make sure you do not try to excuse your actions in any way and that your disclosure is pure gift.

A Deeper Look At Planning Your PhD Apology

1. Don't beat yourself up.
2. When possible go to a quiet place alone; prayer is a good idea.
3. Get quiet.
4. Be present.
5. "Remove your sandals" and get humble.
6. Recognize what you did wrong; it's also valuable think about why this happened so that you can prepare yourself to act differently if this situation comes up again in the future.
7. Imagine how it made your child feel.
8. Sit with the quiet and allow a personal story about yourself come to your awareness. Be vulnerable. It might be a story that doesn't make you look good. It might be a great memory of a time with your child. Be sure to explain why it was so important and significant to you. Your purpose here is to share on a deep human level.
9. Physical props like photo albums may help unearth meaningful stories.

How to deliver your PhD Apology

Once you have planned and prepared your PhD Apology, it's time to share it with your child.

1. **Take off your sandals in humility.** Do not approach your child until you have arrived at the heart place where you are gifting them and it's not about you. Beware your ego: saying, "See how good I am because I'm giving this great big intentional apology." I often pray when trying to humble myself, because it's the best way I know to I rip myself out of my massive ego into sweet humility.

2. **Approach calmly and reverently.** You are now treading upon the sacred space of the relationship.

3. **Ask, "Do you have a minute?" Or gently say, "I need to talk to you."** Patiently engage and get eye contact. Don't exasperate your child further by demanding their immediate attention. They may not be at a place where they can hear you yet. Sometimes you can bridge that rift with extravagant vulnerability, but respect where they are and wait until they are ready to hear you.

4. **Establish equal posture.** Try to get your face on the same level as theirs. If you are speaking from a position above them, there's an unconscious sense of authority assigned to the higher speaker that contradicts your attempts at humility.

5. **Be present, stay present.** This is a reminder to get present and stay present. Your child may not be ready to lovingly receive and accept this gift that you have so vulnerably prepared for her. Are you catching the vulnerability theme? If you skip the vulnerability, you forfeit much of the potential value of your apology.

6. **Admit what you did wrong.** These are the first vulnerable words. No excuses, no long-winded explanations, just come clean and own it.

7. **Acknowledge that you hurt them.**

8. **Say, "I'm really sorry."** Mean it. Really.

9. **Disclose and go deep.** Share a piece of yourself that they have never heard before. Go deep. That is why reflection and preparation is so important. Find a story from your past that reveals some imperfection, some fear, some struggle you had at their age, or any other age. Share a special memory you treasure about your child. Of course, the story always has to be age appropriate. The goal is to humble yourself deeply with your words and your heart. Think about what you would have wanted your parent to say to you if the same thing had happened to you when you were a child.

10. **Say, "I love you."**

11. **Dispel any potential fears your screw-up may have awakened.** Let your child know, "I'm never going to stop loving you no matter what you or I do."

12. **Ask forgiveness.** Say, "Please forgive me." I have focused on humbly apologizing as the first step in making something right and seeking forgiveness, and that is the most important part. I encourage you to add the request, "Please forgive me." This will model the value and importance of forgiveness.

13. **If appropriate, hug them.** Don't force this. Keep it about them: the hug is for them, not for you. Don't relax into receiving mode because it feels good to be hugging and to have this behind you. Keep saying in your head, "I love you. I love you. I love you." Your child will receive the hug much more powerfully if your focus and intention is fully on them. It's okay to cry. Man or woman. Real tears are the highest gift of vulnerability.

14. **Stay in humility the whole time,** even after you say your apology, whether they are open to receiving it or not. Your child may respond angrily, so prepare yourself to be an actor, not a reactor. If they are not ready to accept your apology and say unkind words, it may be helpful to say in your head, "Listen. Listen. Love. Love." Be ready for this and choose to stay in humility. Part of vulnerability is refusing to raise your own sword in defense. If they are still mad they will eventually tire of slashing at an opponent who refuses to pick up her sword and defend herself. It will be hard for them to keep viewing you as an opponent because opponents fight back, and you are not fighting back.

The apology is a gift and we never give gifts with the expectation that the recipient will give anything back to us.

RESTORING

If your car gets a flat, you can have the tire repaired at a gas station, but even after it is repaired, it will still be flat. You have to restore it to its previous condition by filling it with air. The same is true with your relationships. Once you begin to repair a relationship with the appropriate authentic apology, you then need to restore the balance in your child's Positive Relationship Savings Account.

The best way to restore is to move forward and be the best parent possible. Ultimately you will want to go back and rebuild connection and rapport.

Right now, focus on how you are going increase the balance in your child's Positive Relationship Savings Account. You can choose to bury them with joy and overwhelm them with positive attention, interactions and memories. But never be cheesy or insincere; always be present and authentic. That's an option you have every day, in all of your relationships.

Resetters are great for lifting the emotion of the scene.

SMILE RESETTERS

Sometimes your desired outcome may simply be to share a fun interaction with your child, which is a very noble outcome and a good way to start restoring the balance. You aren't looking to discover any information about their life, and you are not trying to communicate anything specific to them. You just want to have fun with them. Here's a story about a time I used a Smile Resetter with a new student to the school:

"Get back on the curb!" I yelled across the parking lot to keep a new student from walking out into the bus lane. He jumped back up on the curb and followed the other students, who glanced back at him curiously.

I was worried that he might have taken my concern for his safety the wrong way, and I didn't want this interaction to negatively flavor his first day at a new school. So I sought him out at lunchtime. He was standing with another student near the fence. I introduced myself and asked Alex how his morning had gone. He shrugged with perfect teenage indifference. Alex wasn't mad at me, but he was wary.

"Put one of your hands out like mine," I said as I stuck both my hands out in front of me palms down. He eyed me suspiciously.

"Come on, put your hand out like this."

He reluctantly did it, and I slid my hands forward until I had a hand to the left and right of his. It looked as though our three hands were resting on an invisible plank.

"Now, watch closely." With palms down, I began to move my hands around his as though they were shells in a con man's shell game. He flinched and pulled back, a little fearful that this might be one of those slapping games. But he relaxed as he realized that I was not going to slap him. I continued repositioning my hands around his hand, over and under, reversing direction, pausing briefly, and then reversing again. He concentrated on my hands, trying to figure out what I was doing, and stole the occasional glance at my face.

After about ten seconds my hands came to a sudden stop. He looked up at me. "Okay, which one is yours?" I said, quite seriously.

His brow scrunched up in a you-can't-be-serious look, and then he jerked his hand down as he realized I was just playing. I threw the kind of huge grin at him that said, "I'm not making fun of you – I am sharing fun with you." He then smiled back in understanding.

I turned to his new friend, who was laughing, and said, "Oh, you think you can do better?" He knew this was silly, but wanted a piece of the fun, too.

I had a client who was so excited to learn about Smile Resetters that she bolted out of the training session early to race home and try it with her high-school-aged daughter. They had been butting heads a lot, caught in a pattern of reacting, and she saw in Smile Resetters a path to the fun interaction that she so desperately craved to have with her daughter. At the end of the training I drove to her house with her husband. She met me at the door with the most excited and joy-filled look on her face. She grabbed my hands and gushed, "It worked! It worked just like you said it would!" And then she proceeded to describe how she had used the Hand Shell Game resetter with her daughter and her friend. She was ecstatic! She had felt stuck in an endless loop of conflict, and now she had discovered a secret escape route that led to fun and positive interactions with her daughter. No longer helpless, she had put an end to suffering from "I-don't-know-what-to-do Syndrome". I gave her another way: a way to have a fun interactions with her children even when their relationships were in a strained season.

The cool thing about Smile Resetters is that they clearly have no parental agenda. It's just fun. And just-fun moments can lead to some of the fondest family memories ever.

Smile Resetters say to your child:

➡ there are loads of mature parent responsibilities I could focus on right now, but I'm choosing to ignore them

➡ I am making my needs unimportant

➡ I am focusing on you

➡ I am making you most the important thing in my life right now

➡ it's okay to share silly moments of pure fun

Not only do Smile Resetters create magic out of an ordinary moment, they also open doors that you can't open any other way. When kids tune in to the fact that you are having fun just to have fun, the unexpected joy of that intention can launch them into a higher level of fun. Their brain says, "I know I'm a kid and it's my job to be on the lookout for fun in every moment, but OMG, this is being provided unexpectedly to me, by my dad or my mom!"

I've got to warn you, these types of behaviors can become seriously addictive.

SUSPEND JUDGMENT

Your child has done something that you disapprove of and you need to assess the situation and determine the appropriate, prudent response. Suspending judgment is especially helpful when high-intensity emotions are involved. When emotions are intense, your immediate goal has to be to strip the emotion out of the scene. Suspending judgment in these situations helps you focus on resetting yourself and your child to restore calm to the situation. Only then can you return to that place of connection where you can have a discussion, give calm directions, and give correction or consequences as appropriate.

Separate the behavior from the child, and remember that most behaviors happen for a reason, which may not be obvious at the moment — especially with teens and preteens. Suspending judgment may also help you to keep a "30,000-foot view" of the whole situation. You are not dismissing the action or any necessary consequences — you are just making a higher, mature decision to postpone a potentially volatile interaction while tempers are roaring.

There are several reasons why suspending judgment until everyone is calm is a practical decision for you to make. When both of you are calm, consequences have more potential value for several reasons:

➡ when you are calm, you invite the child to be calm and you remove the escalation ladder for them to rail against and climb up

➡ the consequence you assign is more likely to be appropriate and related to the poor behavior

➡ the child is less likely to view his consequences as a personal attack

➡ the opportunity for a teachable moment increases greatly

➡ the child is more likely to learn from the situation

➡ if the child learns a new something new, a new distinction, they are less likely to repeat unproductive behaviors in the future

FORGIVE

> You screw up: apologize and ask forgiveness
>
> They screw up: forgive

Can you remember a time when someone hurt you? It's amazing how long we store those hurts and how easily most of us can gain access to those memories. Okay, now think of a great memory involving ice cream ... and now another ice-cream memory. You will probably have too many to choose from, because clearly there can be no such thing as bad ice-cream memories!

I remind you of the power of memories only to encourage you to maximize the number of great memories your kids will have and minimize unnecessary negative ones. Let's spend some time looking at the value of forgiveness in memory creation and maintenance. Giving and receiving forgiveness are the two grandest of all resets. Forgiveness is a relationship reset. It can lead to radically improved interactions and relationships. It can erase or begin to erase scars, repair rifts in a relationship, and restore connection. And forgiveness is a two-sided wonder. You can give forgiveness and you can ask for forgiveness.

Give yourself the gift of forgiveness

Forgiving your kids is all about what it does for you, and only indirectly about what it does for your kids. Most parents who I have deep parenting conversations with admit that they sometimes resent their kids, and even feel badly toward them. I've come to believe that this is pretty universal amongst parents. However, when a child angers you, offends you, or hurts your feelings — it's going to happen — there is monumental value in forgiving and in asking for forgiveness.

Choosing to withhold forgiveness from your child (or anyone) only hurts you; it does not hurt the other person. A wise woman once said that holding someone in unforgiveness is like trying to hurt the other person by slowly drinking poison yourself. When you forgive you choose to give yourself the gift of letting go of anger and resentment.

When your kids hurt your feelings, and you realize that you feel hurt, choose to give *yourself* the benefit of forgiving *them*. Don't carry around that resentment.

A simple recipe for forgiveness

Here is a simple way to forgive your kids and develop your forgiveness muscle.

Physiology:
Take a few forgiveness breaths, slow and deep. Stand tall and stretch your spine to relax your carriage.
Focus:
Silently say to yourself, "I forgive you." Say it over and over.

Forgiveness is an active choice. You can choose to focus on the hurts, the wrongs, the disobedience, the embarrassment, or you can choose to focus on rebuilding the relationship. Keep forgiveness your focus, and don't focus on the hurt. It's difficult, but it is ultimately always your choice — and it provides a huge ROI for your child's Positive Relationship Savings Account.

Be careful that you don't announce your forgiveness to your child with the wrong intention, just to rub it in their face that they hurt you. Even when your kids legitimately hurt your feelings, you still need to be the adult. It sucks, I know, but you can do it!

Consider doing a monthly or quarterly forgiveness inventory to see what junk you need to clear up. Think of it as regular maintenance, like changing the oil in your car. At the very least, do it when you notice that you're harboring resentment towards someone.

When kids apologize to you, you can also model forgiveness by telling them that you forgive them too with the simple words, "Thank you, I forgive you." And then you have to forgive them!

CLOSING

CHAPTER 13

Can a Joke Really Change a Life?

C ONGRATULATIONS, YOU DID IT! STILL, WE'RE NOT QUITE DONE YET. LET'S TAKE a quick look at how far you've already come.

In the **Preset**, you learned that every child's mood has a discrete emotion recipe comprised of only two ingredients.

In the **Reset**, you discovered simple and powerful ways to change a child's mood by changing one or both of the ingredients in their emotion recipe.

> Change the ingredient Ⅲ▶ Change the emotion recipe
>
> Change the emotion recipe Ⅲ▶ Change the emotion (mood)

You learned how to transform undesirable moods, how to strip the emotions out of a scene with the calming power of the Dimmer Switch, and how to leverage Resetology™ to connect with kids and strengthen relationships.

Finally, in the **Mindset**, you learned the relationship habits that allow you maximize the balance in your child's Positive Relationship Savings Account, and to minimize the need for resetting.

THERE'S ALWAYS ANOTHER WAY!

We have spoken quite a bit about the frustrating situations that impose themselves on your life as a parent. In the midst of those challenging situations it's easy to convince yourself that you are out of options. You may find yourself looping on thoughts like:

➡ "I don't know what else to do."
➡ "There's nothing else I can do."
➡ "I'm out of options."

Those thoughts can make you want to give up and prevent you from finding (or even looking for) other possibilities. In the banking world, if you give up early on your savings plan, they slap you with a substantial penalty for early withdrawal of funds and you have to pay a higher fee. The same is true if you give up in those frustrating situations that you encounter with your children: you pay a big price and risk withdrawing massive amounts from your child's PRSA.

Embedded deeply within Resetology™ is the belief that *there is always another way*. Or more accurately, a thousand other ways. Remembering this will allow you to remain resourceful and creative in times that previously would have been difficult to do so.

A corollary to this is the belief that there's a solution to everything — eventually. Firmly grasping this thought will keep hope alive and prevent you from despairing. Best of all, it's true. There really is a solution to everything. In the craziest of situations I faced as a principal, I always knew with certainty that I could figure out a way to fix it. And I always did.

It's been my humble honor and privilege to share my insights and experiences with you. I hope that they have served you well.

I've saved one story for last to highlight the powerful impact that even the smallest elements of Resetology™ can have on a child.

A year ago I got a call from a former student who got in touch with me through the district office. I recognized his name immediately, which meant that Brian had been a frequent flyer in my office.

When I called him back, he told me that he went to the middle school where I was principal and asked if I remembered him. I told him I did. He reminded me that he was in my office all the time (I had already figured that out). Brian said that his dad was an alcoholic and that what little money they had his dad gambled away. So, not surprisingly, Brian was always angry.

Mr. House, I was in your office a lot. I was pissed off all the time. We were very poor and my dad was an alcoholic and a gambler. We bounced between cheap motels and I spent some nights in a Crown Vic. You tried to get me to talk to you. I wouldn't talk to you at all when you asked me questions. But I listened. You talked to me about where my choices would lead me — and how different choices would lead me to different paths.

And then one day you told me a joke. I didn't want to laugh — I tried so hard not to laugh, but I eventually did. And that's when you broke through my walls.

I now have a good job, I'm married and have a three-year-old son. I was telling my wife about my hard past the other day, and she asked me what turned my life around. I'm calling you because I told my wife, "If there is one person I can give credit to for turning my life around, it's Mr. House." You helped me get through my walls.

I thanked Brian for sharing his story with me and told him that I was very proud of him. I was curious what masterpiece of joke-telling I had woven for him, so I asked him if he remembered the life-changing joke. Here it is ...

Q. How do you get a one-armed man out of a tree?

A. *You wave to him.*

I wish you love and laughter!

— Jim

➡ ENGAGE:
I care about your success: Share your stories with us

I wrote this book because I truly care about you and your success. I want to hear about your progress – I want to celebrate your successes with you, and I want to support you in your challenges.

There are a couple reasons why **sharing your stories of resetting will benefit you personally:**

By taking the time to reflect on your experience and capturing it in words or video, you will reinforce your success. This will accomplish two powerful outcomes:

1. You will strengthen your own resetting techniques and your Resetology™ Mindset. Much like how teaching a skill or a concept to someone else strengthens your own understanding and proficiency.

2. You will also increase your likelihood of resetting and acting, not reacting.

Every story submitted will receive a personal thank you message from me.

Submit stores/videos at http://www.resetology.com/share-your-story

CHAPTER 14
The Vault

NSIDE THIS VAULT YOU ARE GOING TO FIND SIMPLE STEP-BY-STEP INSTRUCTIONS for using 8 Resetters. I call them Cheat Sheets.

RESETTER CHEAT SHEETS
1. Invisible Beach Ball Tai Chi
2. Epoxy Grip
3. Cartoon High Five
4. Giant T
5. Do the Ninja
6. 100 Steps
7. Sci-Fi Fingers
8. Elbow-Flex Launch

LARGER FONT CHEAT SHEETS PDF
The font is pretty small on these Cheat Sheets, but don't worry--you can download a larger, full-page version of these Cheat Sheets on the Resetology Resources page.

There are also some bonus Resetter Cheat Sheets there! Check back frequently because these bonus Cheat Sheets will change periodically.

Download the Cheat Sheets and other valuable resources at http://www.resetology.com/book/downloads

RESETTER CHEAT SHEET: Invisible Beach Ball Tai Chi

What to do

Have the child mimic/mirror your movements as you do Tai Chi-like moves holding an invisible beach ball.

➡ Pick up an invisible beach ball (basketball size or larger). Have the child do the same.
➡ Tell him to mimic/mirror your movements.
➡ Hold the ball between your hands, arms extended straight out, chest high.
➡ Push the ball straight up over your head.
➡ Pretend that your upper body is the minute hand on a clock and your waist is the pivot point. Slowly rotate to the right (bending at the waist) in a large circle, brushing the floor with the ball.
➡ Pause when you come back overhead, and then repeat.
➡ Reverse direction every couple of circles.
➡ Finish by compacting the ball down to golf-ball size. Hold the ball up in the palm of your hand and then "flick it" with your fingers or "blow it" into oblivion.

Tips

You have to pretend that you are actually squeezing an invisible beach ball between your hands. Otherwise, the kids will be less inclined to mimic you enthusiastically. Make sure they are holding their own invisible beach balls in the same manner before you begin.

Assume the serious face of a Tai Chi master, or make funny faces and have the kids mimic those as well.

You can add variations as long as the child is still with you.

Add cooing or martial arts movie noises to make it more fun – if appropriate in the space where you are.

Feel free to make up your own beach ball moves!

This works well with groups of children, too.

RESETTER CHEAT SHEET: Epoxy Grip

What to do
Pretend that the child will not let go of your hand after a handshake.

➦ Extend your hand to the child as you normally would when shaking hands.
➦ Shake hands, make eye contact, and smile! Say hello, introduce yourself, etc.
➦ Pretend to let go of their hand, and discover your hand won't come free. (Be careful not to hurt them.)
➦ Look surprised ("Why aren't you letting go?").
➦ Pull your hand towards you as though trying to pull your hand free, but do not let go of their hand.
➦ Look confused.
➦ "Try" to pull your hand free with your other hand.
➦ Put a look of intense effort upon your face (as though trying to rip your hand free from an evil superhero's grasp.)
➦ Carefully shake and move the clasped hands back and forth as though you are still struggling to free your hand.
➦ Pretend that through sheer force you finally overcome them and manage to rip your hand free. (Carefully!)
➦ Shake your newly released hand in relief.

Tips
Important: When you first clasp their hand, slide your hand forward, thumb to thumb, and grasp their palm, instead of grabbing their fingers. This will allow you to carefully grip their hand firmly without hurting them.

Optional: If you are safely able, you can crescendo to a dramatic finish by lifting one foot up to your grip as though you were pushing with your leg for added leverage to "rip" your hand free.

Watch closely, and **DO NOT hurt them.**

You can actually use this Resetter over and over, with the same child – just tone down the intensity. It is very resistant to the Law of Familiarity.

While this works really well with children, you can even pull this off *briefly* with teens and preteens by using the element of surprise and releasing quickly after you feign being stuck.

RESETTER CHEAT SHEET: Cartoon High Five

What to do

Pretend that a child's high five really hurt you – VERY exaggeratedly!

➡ Hold your hand up in the widely recognized invitation to give someone a "high five" – arm extended towards the other person (approximately shoulder high) with palm facing the other person (as in a traffic cop's "stop" gesture, only with elbow bent and relaxed – not rigid).

➡ Say: "Give me a high five!"

➡ When they slap your hand, recoil dramatically as though it really hurt.

➡ Put a cartoonish look of surprise and pain on your face

➡ Shake your hand rapidly as though you were trying to shake water off it.

➡ Say: "Wow, I didn't know you were so strong!"

➡ Turn your hand over and look at the palm and pretend there is an invisible softball in your hand. Squeeze the ball and relax it over and over. This will give the impression that your hand is throbbing like an injured character in an old Saturday morning cartoon.

Tips

Younger kids will probably want to repeat it again and again. This has been hugely successful for me and kids will run up to me and hold their hand out in anticipation of exercising their "super-hero high five power".

If they are being stubborn (they know how to do a high five but are exercising control by not participating) sometimes I will counter-offer with, "How about a 'high two'?" while holding up two fingers. If they still don't respond I may offer a "high three" or a "high seven" to try to break through. Voice and face variations can help a lot, too.

For those kids that want to do this every time they see me, I use a quasi random-reward schedule: sometimes I let them give me a high five, other times I may say I'm still recovering from the last time. (All tongue-in-cheek, of course.)

In future interactions you can choose to vary your "pain-reaction" in an endless variety of ways: shaking your whole arm wildly, sending tremors through your entire body, spinning around, bobbing your head, etc.

RESETTER CHEAT SHEET: Giant T

What to do

Guide the child step-by-step to assume the posture of a standing, smiling, human "T".

Say each step out loud as you do the same thing yourself:

1. I want to see if you can do something. Okay: do what I do.
2. Stand up TALL. Like me.
3. Put your arms out to your sides (making a big T, or Y).
4. Look up at the ceiling.
5. Put a BIG smile on your face.
6. Bounce up and down on your toes, like this.

Tips

Pause briefly after each step to see if the child is mimicking your movements. Then proceed to the next step.

Be encouraging and affirming ("Look at those nice straight arms!").

This is super simple and surprisingly powerful!

You can even use this silly Resetter to reset yourself!

This Resetter can also be used to teach a preteen, and even teens, how their body affects their emotions. Convince them that you want to show them something valuable about emotions. Then guide them through the steps (without the encouragement). While they are smiling and looking up in the T posture say to them: "Now try to be mad" (or sad, or bored).

RESETTER CHEAT SHEET: Do the Ninja

What to do

Guide the child through a cartoonish version of the martial-art crane position that the Karate Kid made famous in the movie of the same name. Have the child mimic/mirror your movements. Practice this in advance.

1. Stand tall with your feet together.
2. Feel the ground under your feet (this is the starting position).
3. Without moving your feet, shift your weight to your RIGHT foot, then lean to the RIGHT.
4. Return to starting position, then shift your weight to your LEFT foot and lean to the LEFT.
5. Return to starting position. Now lift your LEFT heel so that only your toes are touching the ground. Then lift your whole LEFT foot a few inches off the ground and hold.
6. Return to starting position. Lift your RIGHT heel so that only your toes are touching the ground.
7. Now lift your whole foot a few inches off the ground and hold.
8. With hands at your side, bend knees and lower yourself several inches.
9. Shift and balance all of your weight over one foot.
10. Slowly stand upright on one leg (keep the knee bent in the leg that raises as you stand).
11. Raise your arms slowly as though you were lifting wings high to flap.
12. Point fingers forward.
13. Make martial-arts cooing sound ("Ooooooo!").

Tips

As always, be careful. Choose a safe, flat location to do this Resetter.
Pick either foot.

Option: You can simplify the verbal instructions and just have them silently mimic/mirror you.

If child is athletic say, "Switch!" and change feet by jumping from one foot to the other (be careful!).

RESETTER CHEAT SHEET: 100 Steps

This produces a very quick and radical change in physiology. There are many ways to have a child (or children) do a LOT of full-body movement in a short period of time!

This is effective with just one child or with a group.

Safety directions: "Be careful not to interfere with or touch anyone else!"

What to do

Say: "You only have two minutes to finish this quest. You need to take exactly 100 steps. You can step in any direction. You can change direction as often as you want. BUT you must END UP right back here on your 100th step … "

This Resetter can also be done indoors on stairs (one child on each side of a stairway) or on a playground – in and out of a painted circle or a rectangle.

Count cadence out loud (have kids count with you? just them?).

For YOUNGER kids, change the number of steps – seven, 10, 20, 23?

Tips/Additional Variations
- ➡ Count each step out loud
- ➡ Jump on every 10th step
- ➡ Shout out every 10th step
- ➡ Giant steps
- ➡ Slow-motion steps
- ➡ Carefully change direction every multiple of five/10 steps
- ➡ Change direction only on even numbers
- ➡ With a group, the leader can count out steps to create a cadence; leader can say odd numbers and kids shout out evens
- ➡ Six steps outside of the circle, then four steps inside the circle and repeat
- ➡ Follow the leader with series of four to six steps
- ➡ Partner up

Setting a time challenge increases their pace. Good for quick and radical resetting!

RESETTER CHEAT SHEET: Sci-fi Fingers

What to do

Sci-fi Fingers "V"

1. Hold up your right hand in the swearing-in gesture
2. Make a V by splitting the four fingers — two fingers on each side

Sci-fi Fingers "W"

1. Start with Spock Fingers
2. With two middle fingers stuck together, pull the two outside fingers away from the two middle fingers, forming a "W" with 4 fingers (ignore the thumb)

Putting it all together

1. Challenge them to copy your "V"
2. Then once they are close to mastering the "V", challenge them to copy your "W"
3. Then while they are trying to do that, switch rapidly back and forth between the V and W.
4. Stay just a bit ahead of their competence — master this yourself first.

Tips

It will help you to practice this ahead of time so that you can demonstrate what the "V" and "W" actually look like.

RESETTER CHEAT SHEET: Elbow-Flex Launch

An unusual and amusing way to launch small objects a short distance!
Be cautious and aware of the surroundings – be careful that nothing can be broken. Use something fairly lightweight in order to control the launch. It may be better to teach this outdoors.

What to do
Set up:
1. Make a fist.
2. Place a small/light object in the saddle between your forearm and bicep.
3. Squeeze the object inside the saddle.
4. Right fist is touching/almost touching the right shoulder (or left fist/left shoulder).

To launch:
1. Rapidly straighten arm – the resulting motion will launch the object cradled.
2. Don't hyper-extend elbow.

Now teach them.

Tips
With very little practice, you will be able to control direction, angle, altitude, velocity and distance quite successfully!
With a little more practice you can even aim your object.
Suggested launch items: ping pong ball; tennis ball; any small lightweight ball; bundled socks; wine cork.

Acknowledgements

THERE IS SO MUCH GRATITUDE TO SPREAD AROUND BECAUSE SO MANY PEOPLE have their fingerprints on this book in some way — a giant heart-felt thank you to ALL of you — especially those I forgot to mention here.

I am blessed with the kind of family that that usually exists only in myth and legend. Thanks Mom and Dad (I already gushed about you in the dedication — go back and read it); Lori (my favorite sister, you have always led by example — and no, mom didn't make me say that); Will (my best friend on the planet — you probably don't know how much you inspire me); DeAnn (my favorite sister-in-law — so smart, talented, and a great mom!); and Rachel (my FAVORITE niece ... High Five!). Not enough space here to convey how much I love you all, and how privileged I am, and have always been, to be loved back by you!

The JOY of God is my strength. No mistaking where this book comes from.

Dick Van Dyke and Bill Cosby: When I was just a lad, your collective genius ignited and unleashed my imagination and propelled my ability to Find the Fun in most any situation. You've given me a lifetime of smiles, and by extension, are helping me to create happier, more connected families.

There are two people who invested a ridiculous amount of time in this book. They helped form me as a writer, and helped shape this manuscript — years in the making. Michael Schrauzer and Jerry Guern: I owe you a debt of gratitude I can never repay. Viva la Writing Group! John Stenbeck, you arrived late in the writing stages, but your contribution can not be underestimated.

A nod to Tony Robbins who taught me so many things and showed me why what I've done naturally my whole life works so well. You also gave me many new distinctions that helped me to positively impact 1000s of students more effectively.

Jeff Selano, Jim Cargill, Michael Dean, my other brothers, you have been unwavering and relentless voices of encouragement (and pushing) from the beginning. Just thanks.

Pam Hendrickson, you made this bigger just by being the first "big platform" to believe in me and Resetology™.

I still shake my head in wonder, gratitude, and humility at those of you who opened up your wallets, unsolicited, to ensure that this book could be the best it could be, and be read by you and all the others. This would not have been possible without you.

I'm grateful to all of you who participated in my seminars and engaged me as coaching clients — especially the early ones — you helped me to shape Resetology™ to have the greatest impact on parents and families. Special thanks to those of you who generously shared your personal stories in this book for all of us to learn from.

This book has been a journey and I hope I've been faithful in my own growth in the same manner in which the book itself has matured — in ways that put both of us at the service of others.

Working by myself all day long for years, creating something new has been the single biggest challenge of my life. All of you who offered smiles, asked with genuine interest, and offered encouragement sustained me more than you will ever know.

Thanks for the foreword, Wes Schaeffer — I so appreciate your sense of humor, your faith, the inspiring dedication to your family, and your amazing business expertise. Thanks for believing in me and I look forward to continuing to learn from you.

Every author blessed to work with a gifted editor bows in reverence to the magical ways that she impacts and improves the book. Sally Collings, you skillfully put me through my paces and in the end the book emerged so much better because of you!

All of the staff and students at all of the schools ... I am honored to have worked with you.

My creative team is unparalleled and I am so blessed to work with all of you — JP, Chelsey, and Michael. I dream it big and you create it even better!

I am humbled, grateful, excited, and I love you all.

And just in case you are reading this, Sandra Bullock, my calendar actually does have an opening for lunch. And Dick Van Dyke, singing Lida Rose with you and the Vantastix is on my bucket list!

Referral Shout-outs

MY PRODUCTION TEAM

I was privileged and blessed to collaborate with some incredibly talented people as I prepared to send this book (and its mission to help families) out into the world.

Michael Schrauzer (www.MichaelSchrauzer.com)

Michael was massively influential in the shaping of this content within our writing group, and he is solely responsible for the entire interior design and layout. I could not be more excited about how the book looks on the inside! If you want your book to look like a best-seller when readers open it up, Michael is the gifted designer you are looking for.

Chelsey Marie (wwwChelseyMarie.com)

Chelsey is a super-smart branding expert and website master builder! She has the ability to take my ideas and instantly make them better in every conceivable way! And then she stretches me with her razor-sharp marketing sense. It's now a fact of life, people judge you by your website, and you get one chance to make a first impression.

Justin Panlasigui (www.JPArtistry.com)

People DO judge a book by its cover, and I am enormously proud of the cover that Justin created for this book. This guy is magic! I say to him, "I want a realistic-looking alarm pull that says RESET instead of fire — DONE! He also created the kinetic typography (moving-text video) from "Jim's Story" on Resetology.com. Instant high-level credibility!

Ryan Palasigui (www.TwoStopFilms.com)

Ryan and his company are responsible for creating the Book Trailer video for this book, and many of the shorter Resetology videos. The work speaks for itself! SUPER talented!

Pam Hendrickson (MarketingRoadmap.com)

I've learned so much from Pam! She inspired me greatly when she saw the value of Resetology and then contributed a story to the book. If you are writing a book, Pam will show you how to get noticed, connect, and build a relationship with your readers — all with huge integrity.

Note: None of these über-talented folks are inexpensive … but if you are looking for top-drawer, ridiculously talented professionals to collaborate with on your project, I encourage you to connect with them.

— Jim

Hire Jim to Speak

Bring Jim to your company, your conference, or your special event!

Jim is an engaging speaker and his presentations are fresh and powerful. He has the ability to quickly connect with his audience, gain their trust, understand their needs, and then guide them to new skills and understandings.

Jim also leads exciting and productive Resetology™ trainings designed to equip your group with the confidence to handle challenging situations in powerful new ways!

Please visit www.Resetology.com for information about The Reset™ Academy and one-on-one coaching.

Speaking, Seminars & Coaching!

Made in the USA
San Bernardino, CA
30 August 2014